DINKY TOYS SETS AND GIFT SETS

Alan Spree

AMBERLEY

First published 2026

Amberley Publishing
The Hill, Stroud
Gloucestershire, GL5 4EP

www.amberley-books.com

ISBN 978 1 3981 2959 7 (print)
ISBN 978 1 3981 2960 3 (ebook)

British Library Cataloguing in Publication Data.
A catalogue record for this book is available from the British Library.

Typesetting by SJmagic DESIGN SERVICES, India.
Printed in the UK.

Appointed GPSR EU Representative: Easy Access System Europe Oü, 16879218
Address: Mustamäe tee 50, 10621, Tallinn, Estonia
Contact Details: gpsr.requests@easproject.com, +358 40 500 3575

Contents

Introduction

Dinky Toys are very detailed miniature representations and with only a few exceptions most models were included in sets even though most items could still be purchased separately. At the date of publication Dinky Sets are still highly sought after and can be sold for many thousands of pounds.

This book has been put together with the aim of showing the many sets that have been available since the first Modelled Miniatures became Dinky Toys. A gift set or a set is taken as a boxed set of two or more different models; it does not include trade sets or sets of a number of the same models.

The format of the book is to show the sets in numerical rather than chronological order, although occasionally on a reissue or if the set does not have a number that may not be the case. It is noted that some of the sets of the same number were sold with models of a different colour or indeed different models. Where possible this has been indicated in the text. This book is not intended as a definitive work on Dinky Toy sets.

The book shows the diverse range of models including human and animal figures, train sets, commercial vehicles, passenger cars, military models, aeroplanes, ships, racing cars, farmyard equipment, emergency vehicles, television and film vehicles and even doll's house furniture.

I acknowledge that issues of *Meccano Magazine* and Dinky Toys catalogues have proved invaluable in determining information on what sets were available and in some cases the size and the original issue price of the models.

A Short History of Dinky Toys

Pre-war Production From 1933

Frank Hornby established Meccano in 1901 to make metal erector construction sets and produced these at the Binns Road factory in Liverpool, and later also produced Hornby Train sets and accessories named Modelled Miniatures which later became Dinky Toys in December 1933. The Dinky Toys were produced both in Liverpool and Bobigny in France. The Second World War brought production to a standstill for several years. By this time both branches had produced cars, trucks, buses, military vehicles, aircraft, ships and accessories of various kinds.

Post-war Production 1945 to 1980

Pre-war stocks were put on the market in time for the 1945 Christmas season, but no new production took place until 1946 when many models were reissued. The first notable changes occurred later in 1946 with the introduction of more realistic cast hubs with a raised central section. The first entirely new post-war model, a Jeep, appeared in 1946. In 1947 the first Dinky Supertoys were issued which had diecast wheel hubs, with a partly concave pattern, and treaded rubber tyres. Until this point, all Dinky tyres had been slick.

The original British numbering system of numbers and letters began to change in January 1954. The 500 series moved to 900 numbers a year later, and some of them were shifted to 400 series numbers by the beginning of 1956. The 1954 British Dinky catalogue gave both numbers; French Dinky Toys were renumbered during 1959. In the British system, one- and two-digit numbers were used for accessories, 100s for cars, 200 to 249 for racing and sports cars, 250 to 299 for public service vehicles, 300s for agricultural vehicles and character cars, 400s for light and medium trucks, 600s for military vehicles, 700s for aircraft and accessories, and 900 numbers for Supertoys, including a few large aircraft. The French Dinky 500 numbers were used for cars and small trucks, with military vehicles, aircraft, Supertoys and accessories in the 800 series.

The 1950s and 1960s saw many changes in Dinky Toys. Clear plastic windows began to appear in 1958. Suspension was introduced in 1959, fingertip steering in 1960 and a wealth of moving and detailed parts in the 1960s. In 1957 the first Dublo Dinky Toys appeared for use on OO-gauge 1:76-scale railroad platforms. Though a few small-scale models had been produced since the 1930s, most Dinky Toys had been built more or less to O gauge: 1:43 to 1:48 scale, with larger vehicles generally made to a slightly smaller scale so as not to look excessively big beside models of smaller vehicles. The Dublo series never really caught on and was withdrawn after a few years. During the 1960s Dinky began to make models to a larger scale, approximately 1:35 instead of 1:43.

In 1963 British Dinky Toys was bought by the Tri-Ang firm, and in the same year the first Dinky antique car, a Model T Ford, was issued. In 1965 six models of US cars were made for Dinky in Hong Kong.

Dinky Speedwheels first appeared in 1969, usually with chromed hub patterns, and appeared on a variety of vehicles. Models of real cars and trucks were joined in growing numbers by vehicles from television and film.

However, all these modes were not enough to keep Dinky Toys solvent. French production ceased in 1972, though the Spanish firm of Pilen manufactured some French Dinky Toys later in the 1970s and Solido made an effort to do the same in 1981. The British branch struggled on until 1980, farming out some production to Polistil in Italy as well as the Universal firm of Hong Kong.

Captions

The information in the captions is generally given in the following format:

Date: 19xx–19xx. As far as can be ascertained the dates advertised for sale.
Length: xxx mm. The length of the model or height as stated.
Body: colour (alternatives).
Price: the initial price where known or price at another date as indicated.
Other: for example, scale or type of hubs, tyres, radiator, type of chassis.

Dinky Gift Sets

No. 1 Station Staff Set Issue One Pre-war Modelled Miniatures

1931–1939. Comprising: Station Master to supervise operations, Ticket Collector for station barrier, Guard with his whistle and flag giving the clearance for the train to pull away, Locomotive Driver with his oil can and two Porters, one with luggage and one without. The figures are enamelled in colour and were designed to add the final touch of realism to the Hornby Railway station platforms. Height 39 mm. Price 3 pence each. Price of complete set 1 shilling 6 pence.

No. 1 Station Staff Set Issue Two

1939–1941. Note that the Guard does not have his hand raised with a whistle in it as in the earlier sets and the models are smaller. Height 35 mm. Price of set 1 shilling 6 pence.

No. 001 Station Staff Set (Renumbered from 1)

1952–1956. Comprising: five of the previous set, Station Master not included. Height 35 mm. Price of set 4 shillings 8 pence.

Railway Accessories No. 1

Comprising: three pieces of miniature luggage and a truck, this was first advertised in *Meccano Magazine* in December 1934 and was to a scale suitable for Hornby Train sets. Price 1 shilling.

Railway Accessories No. 2

Comprising: six milk cans and a truck, this was first advertised in *Meccano Magazine* in December 1934 and was to a scale suitable for Hornby Train sets. Price 1 shilling 3 pence.

Railway Accessories No. 3

Comprising: postbox, platform ticket machine, a metal name-print machine and two benches. First advertised in *Meccano Magazine* in December 1934 and was to a scale suitable for Hornby Train sets. Price 1 shilling 6 pence.

No. 1 Commercial Vehicles Set

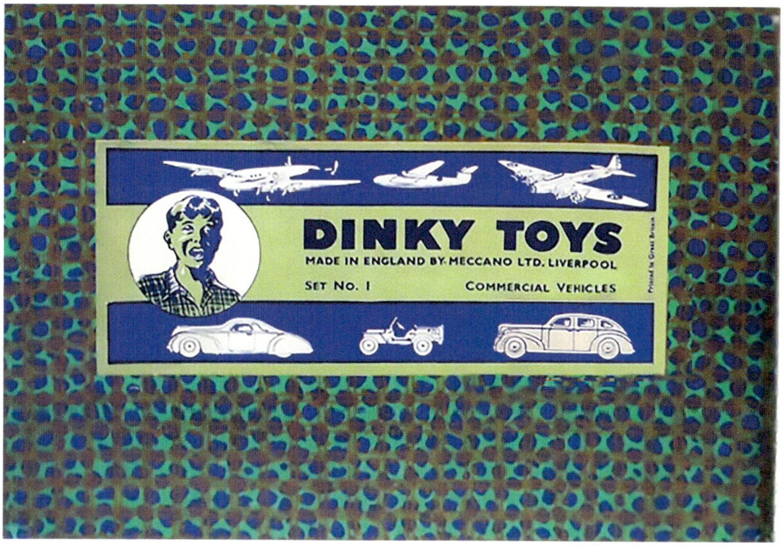

1947–1948. Comprising:

29c Double Deck Bus, first type AEC radiator, cream upper body, red lower body, black ridged hubs. Length 101 mm. 1946 price 2 shillings 3 pence.

25b Covered Wagon, dark green body and tin tilt, black chassis and ridged hubs. Length 105 mm. 1946 price 2 shillings.

25d Petrol Tank Wagon, dark green body no 'Petrol' as in later issues, black ridged hubs. Length 110 mm. 1946 price 2 shillings.

25e Tipper Truck, light grey body, black ridged hubs. Length 105 mm. 1946 price 2 shillings 3 pence.

25f Market Gardener's Lorry, yellow body, black ridged hubs. Length 110 mm. 1946 price 1 shilling 9 pence.

The set is packed in a green box with a cardboard insert. Individual models first introduced in 1934.

No. 1 Farm Gear Set

1952–1954. Comprising:

27a Massey Harris Tractor, red body, yellow wheel hubs, swivel wheels at front. Length 89 mm. Price 5 shillings. Renumbered 300 in 1954.

27b Halesowen Harvest Trailer, brown and red body, tow bar, removable front and back support. Length 121 mm. Price 2 shillings 10 pence. Renumbered 320 in 1954.

27c Massey Harris Manure Spreader, red body, tow bar, working parts at the rear. Length 113 mm. Price 3 shillings 9 pence. Renumbered 321 in 1954.

27g Moto-kart, brown and green body with the rear tipping. Length 110 mm. Price 4 shillings 6 pence. Renumbered 342 in 1954.

27h Disc Harrow, red and yellow body, rotating discs. Length 86 mm. Price 2 shillings 9 pence. Renumbered 322 in 1954.

Price of set 17 shillings 3 pence. Individual models introduced in 1949.

No. 2 Farmyard Animals Set

1932–1954. Comprising: a pair of brown and white horses, price 7 pence the pair, a pair of brown and black and white cows, price 7 pence the pair. One white sheep and one brown pig, price 2 pence each. They were advertised as being useful for placing in lineside fields for the Hornby O gauge railways.

Price for set 1 shilling 6 pence.

No. 002 Farmyard Animals

1954–1956. Comprising: a pair of brown and cream horses, a pair of brown and cream cows, a white sheep and a brown pig. Price 6 shillings 6 pence. It seems that the models were no longer sold separately. For Hornby O gauge.

No. 002 Commercial Vehicles

1952–1954. Comprising:

25m Bedford End Tipper, introduced in 1948, orange red and cream body, handle that tips the rear, hinged tail board. Length 98 mm. Price 5 shillings 9 pence.

27d Land Rover, introduced in 1950, orange body, deep blue interior, driver, red ridged hubs. Length 90 mm. Price 3 shillings 9 pence.

30p Studebaker Tanker 'Esso', introduced in 1952, red body with ESSO MOTOR OIL PETROL on sides, ridged hubs. Length 112 mm. Price 3 shillings 4 pence. Renumbered 422 in 1954.

30s Austin Covered Wagon, introduced in 1952, blue and light blue (maroon and fawn) body, ridged hubs. Length 104 mm. Price 2 shillings 10 pence. Renumbered 413 in 1954.

30n Farm Produce Wagon, introduced in 1950, green and yellow body, ridged hubs. Length 107 mm. Price 3 shillings 3 pence. Renumbered 343 in 1954.

Price of the set 17 shillings 9 pence.

No. 3 Private Automobiles

1946–1948. Comprising a mixture of the following models all with black ridged wheels:

30d Vauxhall, brown body, black chassis, shield shape radiator. Length 98 mm. Price 1 shilling 9 pence.

36b Bentley, green (blue) body, black chassis, Bentley radiator. Length 93 mm. Price 1 shilling 9 pence.

36d Rover, green (blue) body, moulded chassis, Rover radiator. Length 94 mm. Price 1 shilling 9 pence.

38a Frazer Nash, grey (blue) body, moulded chassis, black painted baseplate. Length 82 mm. Price 2 shillings.

38b Sunbeam-Talbot, red (blue, yellow) body, moulded chassis, black painted baseplate. Length 92 mm. Price 2 shillings.

38c Lagonda Sports Coupé, grey (green, maroon) body, moulded chassis, black painted baseplate. Length 92 mm. Price 2 shilling 9 pence.

38d Alvis, green (maroon) body, black painted baseplate. Length 95 mm. Price 2 shillings.

38e Armstrong Siddeley, light grey (cream) body, black painted baseplate. Length 95 mm. Price 2 shillings 6 pence.

38f Jaguar, red (blue) body, black painted baseplate. Length 80 mm. Price 2 shillings 9 pence.

Individual models introduced in 1946 except 36b in 1940.

No. 3 Railway Passengers Wayside Set

1932–1937. Set of Wayside figures comprising: 3a Mother and Child, 3b Businessman, 3c Male Hiker, 3d Female Hiker, 3e Newsboy (running), No. 3f Woman with Luggage. The image below is the 1935 model's advert in *Meccano Magazine* showing the above models. Height 39 mm.

Passengers
Dinky Toys No. 3

No 3a Woman & Child	each 3d.	No. 3d Female Hiker ... each 3d.
No. 3b Business Man	,, 3d.	No. 3e Newsboy ... ,, 3d.
No. 3c Male Hiker ...	,, 3d.	No. 3f Woman ... ... ,, 3d.

Price of complete set 1/6

Modelled Miniatures No. 3
Passengers

The various types of passengers to be seen at any railway station are well represented in Modelled Miniatures No. 3. The set contains six figures as illustrated, comprising Business Man, Male Hiker, Female Hiker, Newsboy, Lady, and Mother and Child.

No. 3 Railway Passengers Second Issue

1937–1939. In an all-plain green box with a card insert showing the figures against the lineside. The Mother with Child now has the child on her left, the Male Hiker is without a stick, the Newsboy is now with a brown tray of papers and the Lady with Luggage is repainted. Hornby O gauge scale. Height 35 mm. Price 3 pence each or 1 shilling 6 pence the set.

No. 003 Railway Passengers (Renumbered from 3)

1952–1956. A new moulding comprising: Mother with Child on her left, Businessman, Male Hiker without stick, Female Hiker, Newsboy with grey tray and a Woman with coat and round case. Hornby O gauge scale. Height 35 mm. Price of set 5 shillings 3 pence.

No. 003 Passenger Cars

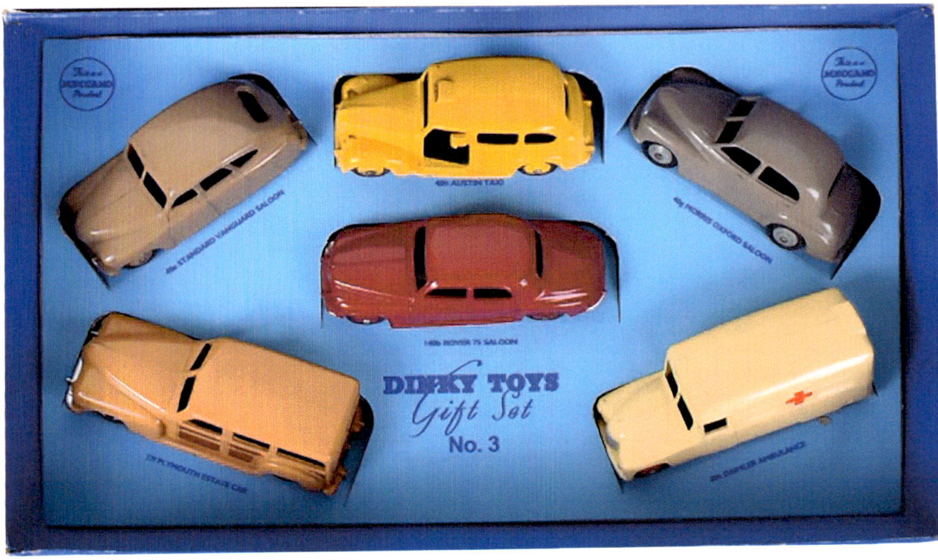

1952–1954. Comprising:

27f Estate Car, fawn (brown) two-tone body, ridged hubs. Renumbered 344 in 1954. Length 105 mm. Price 2 shillings 8 pence.

30h Daimler Ambulance, cream body with red crosses, ridged hubs. Renumbered 253 in 1954. Length 96 mm. Price 2 shillings 8 pence.

40e Standard Vanguard, fawn (blue) body, covered rear wheels, plain boot, ridged hubs. Renumbered 153 in 1955. Length 91 mm. Price 2 shillings 2 pence.

40h Austin Taxi, yellow (blue) body, taxi sign on roof and ridged hubs. Renumbered 254 in 1955. Length 94 mm. Price 2 shillings 11 pence.

40g Morris Oxford Saloon, beige (green) body with ridged hubs. Renumbered 159 in 1955. Length 93 mm. Price 2 shillings 2 pence.

140b Rover 75, maroon body with ridged hubs. Renumbered 156 in 1955. Length 101 mm. Price 2 shillings 2 pence.

Price of set 15 shillings.

Individual models introduced in 1950 except 40H in 1951.

27f Estate Car

30h Daimler Ambulance

40e Standard Vanguard Saloon

40h Austin Taxi

40g Morris Oxford Saloon

140b Rover 75 Saloon

No. 4 Engineering Staff Wayside Set

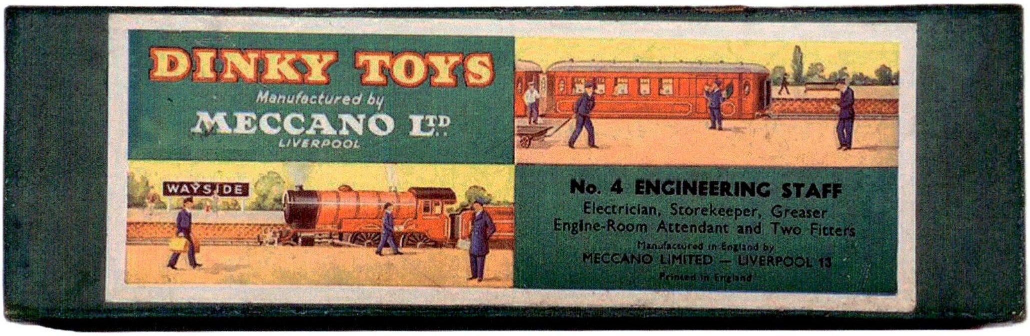

1932–1939. Set of Wayside figures comprising two Fitters, Storekeeper, Greaser and Engine Room Attendant. For use along the line and railway premises, especially stations, engines and yards. Price 3 pence each or 1 shilling 6 pence the set. Height 39 mm.

No. 4 Engineering Staff Second Issue

1939–1941. Comprising: Electrician, two Fitters, Storekeeper, Greaser and Engine Room Attendant, remodelled from previous set. Price 3 pence each. Complete set 1 shilling 6 pence. Hornby O gauge scale. Height 35 mm.

No. 004 Engineering Staff (Renumbered from 4)

1952–1956. Comprising: two Fitters, Store Keeper, Greaser and Engine Room Attendant. The Electrician in the previous set has been omitted. Price 4 shillings 8 pence. Hornby O gauge scale. Height 35 mm.

Below image as described in the 1952 Dinky Toys catalogue.

004 (4)
Engineering Staff
(set of 5) 4/8

No. 4 Racing Cars (Renumbered 243 1955–1959)

1953–1954. Comprising:

23g Cooper Bristol, green body, a cast in driver and a white racing number 6 on the tail. Renumbered 233 in 1954. Length 89 mm. Price 2 shillings 8 pence.

23f Alfa Romeo, green body, a cast in driver and a white racing number 8 on the tail. Renumbered 232 in 1954. Length 100 mm. Price 2 shillings 11 pence.

23h Ferrari, blue body, yellow nose, a cast in driver and a yellow racing number 5 on the tail. Renumbered 234 in 1954. Length 101 mm. Price 2 shillings 11 pence.

23j HWM, green body, cast in driver and a yellow racing number 7 on the tail. Renumbered 235 in 1954. Length 99 mm. Price 2 shillings 11 pence.

23n Maserati, red body, white flash on the nose, cast in driver and a white racing number 9 on the tail. Renumbered 231 in 1954. Length 94 mm. Price 2 shillings 8 pence.

Price of set 12 shillings 6 pence.

Individual models introduced in 1950 except 23j in 1953.

The image below shows the black baseplates with identifying marking.

No. 5 Train and Hotel Staff

1934–1952. Comprising: 1 Pullman Car Conductor, 2 Pullman Car Waiters and 2 Hotel Porters on cream bases. Price 3 pence each. Price of set 1 shilling 3 pence. Hornby O gauge scale. Height 35 mm.

Image below as described in the 1935 Dinky Toys catalogue.

Modelled Miniatures No. 5
Train and Hotel Staff

Five figures are included in this set, including Pullman Car Conductor, two Pullman Car Waiters and two Hotel Porters. The Car Attendants are conspicuous in smart white jackets, and can be used on trains and in stations. The Hotel Porters, in livery, are essentially for use at important stations.

Price, per set, **1/3**

No. 5 Train and Hotel Staff Wayside Set

1932–1937. Set of 5 Wayside figures comprising: 3 Pullman Car Attendants and 2 Hotel Porters. Height 39 mm.

No. 5 Train and Hotel Staff Post-war Set (Renumbered 005)

1952–1956. Comprising: three Pullman Car Attendants in blue and white and two Hotel Porters in brown with different-coloured luggage. Price 4 Shillings 8 pence. Hornby O gauge scale. Height 35 mm.

No. 6 Shepherd Set Pre-war

1934–1952. Comprising:

6a Shepherd wearing a blue smock and hat, holding a crook. Price 3 pence.

6b Black and white collie dog. Price 3 pence.

2d Three sheep white with black marking around the head and legs and one black sheep. Price 2 pence each.

Price of set 1 shilling 2 pence.

No. 6 Shepherd Set Post-war

1954–1956. Comprising:

6a Shepherd wearing a brown smock, a green hat and scarf and holding a crook.

6b Black collie dog.

2d Four white sheep.

Price 4 shilling 4 pence. It seems that the models were no longer sold separately.

No. 6 Commercial Vehicles

1946–1948. Export set for the US market only comprising:

29c Double Decker Bus, introduced in 1946, red (green) body with a cream top, cut-away front mudguard. Does not have stairs as did earlier models. Length 101 mm. Price 2 shillings 10 pence.

29b Streamlined Bus, introduced in 1935, various two-tone cream (grey, green) and red (green, blue) body, rear window. Length 88 mm. Price 1 shilling 4 pence.

25h Streamlined Fire Engine, introduced in 1936, red body. Length 101 mm. Price 1 shilling 9 pence.

30e Bedford Breakdown Truck, introduced in 1946, red (green, grey) body, some models without rear window in the cab. Length 92 mm. Price 1 shilling 8 pence.

30f Ambulance, introduced in 1946, cream (grey) body, black (red) chassis, open window in the cab, red crosses on the side. Length 99 mm. Price 2 shillings.

No. 25h Streamlined Fire Engine

No. 29b Streamlined Bus

No. 29c Double Decker Bus

No. 30e Bedford Breakdown Truck

No. 30f Ambulance

No. 007 Petrol Pump Attendants

007 Petrol Pump Attendants.

1960–1967. Comprising: two plastic figures of Petrol Pump Attendants that came in a polythene bag. Average Height 35 mm. Price of set 10 pence.

No. 008 Fire Station Personnel

1961–1967. Comprising: six plastic figures of fire station personnel in various poses, dark blue and came in a polythene bag with two lengths of white plastic hose. Average height 35 mm. Price of set 3 shillings.

No. 009 Service Station Personnel

1962–1966. Comprising: eight different plastic figures contained in a rigid plastic box with individual compartments and yellow printed card lid. Price 3 shillings 9 pence.

No. 010 Road Maintenance Personnel

1962–1966. Comprising: six plastic workmen, hut, brazier, wheelbarrow and other road-mending accessories. Average height 35 mm. Price 5 shillings.

No. 12 Postal Set

1937–1941. Comprising:

12a GPO Pillar Box, introduced in 1935, red body, GR and Crown markings, sign above in yellow with red Post Office and arrow marking. Height 50 mm. Price 3 pence.

12b Airmail Pillar Box, introduced in 1935, blue body, GR and Crown marking on the body, sign above in blue with white Air Mail markings. Height 50 mm. Price 3 pence.

12c Telephone Call Box, introduced in 1936, red (cream) and silver body, GR and Crown marking on the body, sign above in white with black Telephone markings. Height 62 mm. Price 4 pence.

12d Telegraph Messenger, introduced in 1937, blue body. Height 36 mm. Price 3 pence.

12e Postman, introduced in 1937, blue body. Height 36 mm. Price 3 pence.

34b Royal Mail Van, introduced in 1937, red body, GR, Crown and Royal Mail marking, black roof and bonnet, smooth hubs, white tyres, open rear window, tinplate base. Length 36 mm. Price 10 pence.

Price of set 1 shilling 11 pence.

No. 15 Railway Signals Set

Described in the April 1937 edition of *Meccano Magazine*.

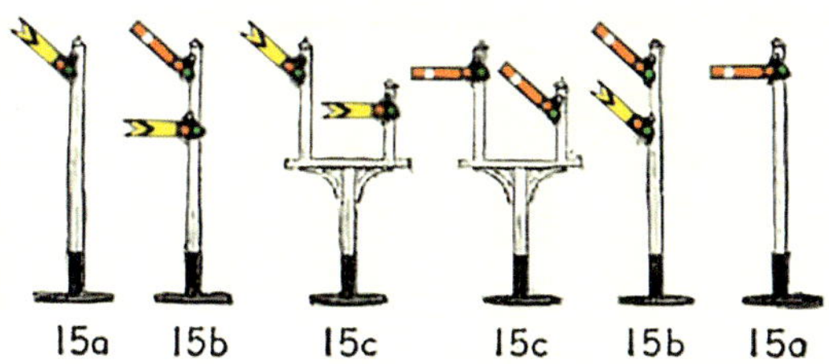

RAILWAY SIGNALS
Dinky Toys No. 15

No. 15a Single Arm Signal. One "Home" and one "Distant" each 2d.

No 15b Double Arm Signal. One "Home" and one "Distant" each 3d.

No. 15c Junction Signal. One "Home" and one "Distant" each 4d.

Price of complete set 1/6

No. 16 Silver Jubilee Train Set Issue 1

1936–1941 Comprising: A4 Loco and Tender with two Coaches in LNER livery, fitted with black smooth hubs, white tyres, illustrated card box with pictorial insert. The set was first advertised in the July 1937 edition of *Meccano Magazine*. The name of the set commemorates the Silver Jubilee of King George V. It has a silver locomotive and coaches with orange (red, blue, dark blue, grey) trim. Also with cream locomotive and coaches with red trim or a blue locomotive and coaches with dark blue trim or a green locomotive and coaches with dark green trim. Price of set 1 shilling 6 pence.

No. 16 Express Train Set (Streamline Train Set) Issue 2 (see also 16 Silver Jubilee Train and 989 Express Passenger Train)

1947–1953. Comprising: blue and black Loco and Tender with two Coaches in LNER livery of brown with grey roofs. The windows on the carriages and the locomotive cab were filled in. Price of set 5 shilling 6 pence.

Pull-along carpet trains featured from the first Hornby Modelled Miniatures Set 21 in 1932, and from 1934 sets 17, 18, 19 and 20 were introduced as Dinky Toys to an approximately 1:76 scale similar to OO scale. These were intended for the younger enthusiast. The sets were originally cast in lead but later examples had a mixture of lead and mazac.

17 Passenger Train Set

1934–1940. Comprising: black and green Loco, green Tender, two green and cream Coaches, or black and maroon Loco, a maroon Tender and two maroon and cream Coaches.

17a Locomotive. Price 9 pence.

17b Tender. Price 5 pence.

20c Two Coaches. Price 7 pence each.

Price of set 2 shillings 3 pence.

No. 18 Goods Train Set

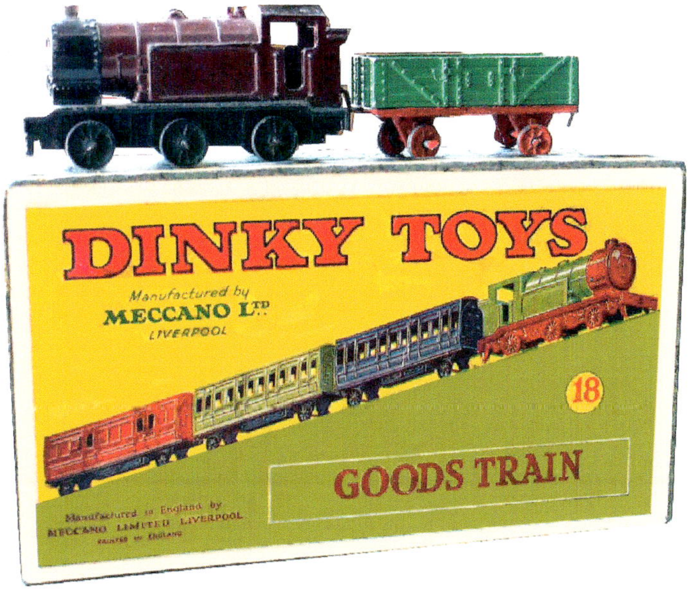

1935-1940. Comprising: 21a black and green (maroon and black) Tank Locomotive. Price 9 pence. 20b three maroon and black Open Wagons. Price 4 pence each. Price of set 1 shilling 9 pence.

No. 19 Mixed Goods Train Set

1935–1940. Comprising:

21a Maroon and black Loco. Price 9 pence.

21b Green and red Open Wagon. Price 4 pence.

21d Red and blue Petrol Tank Wagon. Price 6 pence.

21e Red, yellow and green Lumber Wagon. Price 5 pence. The set came in a blue box with pictorial label to lid. Price of set 1 shilling 11 pence.

No. 20 Passenger Train Set

1935–1940. Comprising:

21a Tank Loco in maroon (green) body with black underbody, roof and nose. Price 9 pence.

20a Two Passenger Coaches in maroon with red base and wheels. Price 7 pence each.

20b Guards Brake Coach in maroon with a red base. Price 7 pence. All coaches have cream roofs. Price of set 2 shillings 6 pence.

No. 21 Hornby Train Set

1932–1935. Comprising:

21a Red and violet blue Tank Locomotive.

21b Green and red Open Wagon.

21c Green and violet blue Crane Truck.

21d Tanker Wagon 'Shell' with blue base and red tank. Price of set 2 shillings and 6 pence. Models have 'Hornby Series' cast into base.

No. 22 Motor Vehicles Set

1933–1935. Comprising:

22a Open Sports Car, red, cream interior and wings, blue wheels. Length 84 mm. Price 6 pence.

22b Closed Sports Coupé, yellow, green roof and wings, yellow effect to wheels. Length 82 mm. Price 6 pence.

22c Motor Truck, powder blue cab and chassis, red rear body, bluish green effect to wheels. Length 90 mm. Price 8 pence.

22d Delivery Van, orange cab and chassis, plain blue van body, red effect to wheels, tinplate radiator surround. Length 83 mm. Price 8 pence.

22e Farm Tractor, mid-blue engine and rear wing assembly casting, yellow engine cover and red wheels. Length 70 mm. Price 9 pence.

22f Army Tank, mid-green with orange turret, hard white rubber tracks. Length 87 mm. Price 1 shilling. Price of complete set 4 shillings.

No. 23 Motor Vehicles Set

1936–1940. Comprising:

23c Mercedes Benz, blue body, white driver, black smooth hubs and tyres. Length 92 mm. Price 8 pence.

23d Auto Union, yellow (red), white driver, racing number 2(1), black tinplate base, black smooth hubs and tyres. Length 100 mm. Price 7 pence.

23e Speed of the Wind, blue, white driver, racing number 1 with blue painted tinplate base, black smooth hubs and tyres. Length 104 mm. Price 8 pence. Also in Blue box. Price of complete set 1 shilling 10 pence.

No. 24 Motor Cars Set

1934–1940. Comprising:

24a Ambulance, cream (grey) body, red chassis, high front wings, red cross marking on side, smooth hubs, white tyres, open windows. Length 102 mm. Price 6 pence.

24b Limousine, blue (red) body, yellow chassis, high front wings, only Type 1 has a spare wheel in the wing, smooth hubs, white tyres, open windows. Length 98 mm. Price 6 pence.

24c Town Sedan, green (blue, cream) body, red chassis, high front wings, only Type 1 has a spare wheel in the wing, smooth hubs, white tyres, open windows. Length 97 mm. Price 1 shilling.

24d Vogue Saloon, blue (green and pink) body, dark blue chassis with high front wings, only Type 1 has a spare wheel in the wing, smooth hubs, white tyres, open windows. Length 107 mm. Price 9 pence.

24e Super Streamlined Saloon, red (green) body, dark red (blue) chassis with high front wings, no spare wheel in either type, smooth hubs, white tyres, open windows. Length 97 mm. Price 9 pence.

24f Sportsman Coupé, cream (yellow) body, blue (brown) chassis with high front wings, only Type 1 has a spare wheel in the wing, smooth hubs, white tyres, open windows. Length 100 mm. Price 9 pence.

24g Sports four-seater Tourer, cream (blue) body, green (black, brown) chassis, high front wings, spare wheel on boot Type 1 only, smooth hubs, white tyres. Length 104 mm with tyre and 98 mm without. Price 1 shilling.

24h Sports two-seater Tourer, green (cream, red) body, black (green) chassis, high front wings, spare wheel on boot Type 1 only, smooth hubs, white tyres. Length 98 mm. Price 1 shilling.

Price of complete set 6 shillings 6 pence.

No. 25 Commercial Motor Vehicles

This set comprises six commercial vehicles that were advertised in the May 1934 edition of *Meccano Magazine* at a price of 9 pence each or the complete set for 4 shillings 6 pence. Over the years four types were produced:

Type 1 Open chassis, tin plate radiator and no lights.

Type 2 Open chassis, die cast radiator with lights.

Type 3 Plain chassis, die cast radiator with lights.

Type 4 Moulded chassis, die cast radiator, lights and bumpers.

25a Wagon, red (grey, cream) body. Length 108 mm. (Type 1), 105 mm (Types 2 and 3) and 110 mm (Type 4).

25b Covered Wagon, blue with cream canvas (grey with grey canvas, green with fawn canvas, green, yellow) body. Length 108 mm. (Type 1), 105 mm (Types 2 and 3) and 110 mm (Type 4).

25c Flat Truck, yellow (green, orange) body. Length 105 mm (Types 1, 2 and 3) and 110 mm (Type 4).

25d Petrol Tank Wagon Esso (Shell BP, Petrol, Power, Mobiloil, Castrol, Texaco, Redline-Glico, Pool), red (green, dark blue, grey) body. Length 108 mm. (Type 1), 107 mm (Type 2), 104 mm (Type 3) and 110 mm (Type 4).

25e Tipping Wagon, maroon and grey (grey, fawn, brown, blue and pink) body. Length 108 mm (Type 1), 105 mm (Types 2 and 3) and 110 mm (Type 4).

25f Market Gardener's Van, green (yellow) body. Length 107 mm (Type 1), 105 mm (Types 2 and 3) and 110 mm (Type 4).

No. 28 Delivery Vans (Reissued as 280)

The No. 28 models were part of a series of eighteen Delivery Vans with advertising print on the body side of the Vans. There were three issues of six different liveried vans per set. Each model had an issue price of 6 pence and a set price of 3 shillings. There were three types of castings:

TYPE 1 CASTING

1933–1935. Type 1 is a two-piece lead body marked with Hornby Series in the earlier issues and Dinky Toys later. They have tin plate radiators and solid wheel and tyre castings which are silver or coloured. Length 84 mm.

TYPE 2 CASTING

1935–1939. Type 2 has a one-piece die-cast body with cast in shield-shaped radiator. They have spats that cover the upper portions of the rear wheels. They have cast smooth wheel hubs with rubber tyres which are normally white. Length 81 mm. All the models carried advertising.

TYPE 3 CASTING

1939–1941. Type 3 has a one-piece die-cast body with cast in rectangular-shaped radiator domed at the top. They have spats that cover the upper portions of the rear wheels. They have cast smooth wheel hubs painted in various colours with black rubber tyres. They have open rear windows. Length 83 mm. All the models carried advertising.

1939–1941. Have cast ridged wheel hubs which are normally black with black rubber tyres and filled-in rear windows. All the models did not carry advertising.

No. 28 Issue 1 Delivery Vans

1934–1940. Comprising:

28a 'Hornby Trains', yellow body.

28b 'Pickfords', royal blue body.

28c 'Manchester Guardian', black cab and chassis, red back.

28d 'OXO', blue body.

28e 'Ensign Cameras', orange body.

28f 'Palethorpes', pale grey blue body.

The models had a Type 1 casting.

No. 28 Issue 2 Delivery Vans (see also 280)

1934–1940. Comprising:

28d 'OXO', mid-blue body, 28g 'Kodak Film', yellow body, 28h 'Dunlop Tyres', red body, 28k 'Marsh's Sausages', dark green body, 28m 'Wakefield Castrol', green body, 28p 'Crawford's', red body. The models had a Type 2 casting.

No. 28 Issue 3 Delivery Vans

1934–1940. Comprising:

28d 'Oxo', blue body, 28h 'Dunlop Tyres', red body, 28m 'Wakefield's Castrol Oil', green body, 28n 'Atco Mowers', green body, 28r 'Swan Pens', black body, and 28w 'Osram Lamps', yellow body. The models had a Type 2 casting.

No. 30 Motor Vehicles

1937–1941. Comprising a mixture of the following models:

30a Chrysler Airflow, green (cream) body with no chassis. Length 103 mm. Price 9 pence.

30b Rolls-Royce, green (grey) body with open chassis. Length 101 mm. Price 9 pence.

30c Daimler, green body with open chassis. Length 98 mm. Price 9 pence.

30d Vauxhall, green (brown, yellow) body with open brown or black chassis and squared radiator. Length 102 mm. Price 9 pence.

30e Breakdown Car, red (green, grey) body with window in rear of cab and a wire hook to the crane. Length 92 mm. Price 9 pence.

30f Ambulance, grey (cream) body with red crosses painted on the sides, red (black) chassis. The chassis is moulded with holes for passengers. It has a plain radiator and all windows are open. Length 101 mm. Price 9 pence.

30g Caravan, two-tone green body with two wheels and a towing bar. Length 81 mm. Price 6 pence.

All models had white tyres and the issue price for the set with the ambulance was 4 shillings 6 pence and with the ambulance replaced by the caravan it was 3 shillings 11 pence. Individual models were introduced in 1935 except 30g, in 1936.

No. 30a Chrysler Airflow

No. 30b Rolls Royce

No. 30c Daimler

No. 30d Vauxhall

No. 30e Breakdown Car

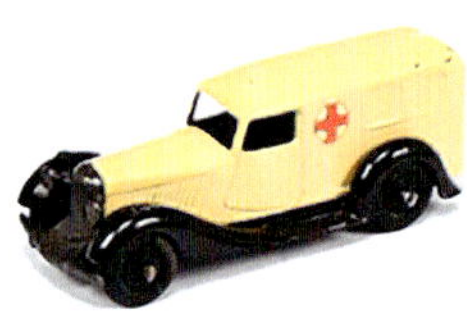

No. 30f Ambulance

No. 30g Caravan

No. 33 Mechanical Horse and Trailers

1935–1937. There were two issues of this set 33/1 with five trailers. Price of set 3 shillings 6 pence and 33/2 with four trailers without 33d Box Van. Price of set 2 shillings 10 pence.

33a Mechanical Horse. Price 6 pence. Length 65 mm.

33b Flat Truck. Price 6 pence. Length 64 mm.

33c Open Wagon. Price 6 pence. Length 64 mm.

33d Box Van. Price 8 pence. Length 70 mm.

33e Dust Wagon. Price 8 pence. Length 61 mm.

33f Petrol Tank (Esso or Wakefield Castrol). Price 8 pence. Length 61 mm.

No. 35 Small Motor Cars

This pre-war set comprises:

35a Austin 7 Saloon with blue (red, grey) body, solid white tyres. Length 51 mm.

35b Racer with silver (blue, yellow, red) body, three issues first without driver and then with, renumbered to 200 in 1954, solid white or black tyres. Length 60 mm.

35c MG 2-seater with blue (red, green) body, solid white or black tyres. Length 52 mm. Price 3 pence each.

Price of set 9 pence.

No. 36 Motor Cars with Drivers, Passenger and Footmen

1937–1940. Comprising:

36a Armstrong Siddeley Saloon, blue (grey) body with a black moulded chassis. No driver. Open windows, Armstrong Siddeley radiator and vertical bonnet louvres. Length 97 mm.

36b Bentley Sports Coupé, yellow (blue) body with a black moulded chassis with holes for passengers and driver. No driver. Open windows, Bentley radiator. Length 100 mm.

36e British Salmson, two-seater, blue (grey) body a dark blue (red) moulded chassis. Driver, with or without a spare wheel at the rear, solid metal windscreen. Salmson radiator. Length 93 mm.

36f British Salmson, four-seater, red (grey) body with dark red chassis, driver, cast in spare wheel, solid metal screen. Salmson radiator. Length 98 mm.

36d Rover Saloon Streamlined, blue (green) body with black (green) chassis, no driver but slot provided. Rover radiator. Length 99 mm.

36c Humber Vogue Saloon, blue (brown, grey) body with blue (black) chassis, no driver. Humber radiator. Length 90 mm.

All contained within yellow base with fold-down flap with details and plain blue lid. An extremely rare box and contents. All with smooth black hubs and white tyres. Price of each model 11 pence with the complete set 5 shillings 6 pence. Individual models introduced in 1937 except 36f, in 1936, and 36c, in 1935.

No.36e British Salmson 2-seater

No.36f British Salmson 4-seater

No.36a Armstrong Siddeley Saloon

No.36d Rover Saloon Streamlined

No.36c Humber Vogue Saloon

No.36b Bentley Sports Coupe

No. 37 and 37a Motor Cyclist Civilian

1937–1941. Comprising: either three or six Civilian Motorcycles each in the following different colours: black, blue, green, white, red and grey, all with solid white tyres. Length of each 45 mm. Price 6 pence each.

No. 39 US Sedans and Coupé Cars (and then issued as Set 2 Private Automobiles)

1946–1948. This US export set comprises:

39a Packard Super 8, green (brown) body with moulded half tyre, three windows each side, black painted baseplate: Length 107 mm.

38b Oldsmobile 6, grey (blue green brown) body, black painted baseplate, two windows each side. Length 107 mm.

39c Lincoln Zephyr, grey (green) body, black painted baseplate, one window each side. Length 106 mm.

39d Buick Viceroy, grey (maroon) body, moulded full tyres, three windows each side, black painted baseplate. Length 103 mm.

39e Chrysler, cream (blue yellow) body, three windows each side, black painted baseplate. Length 106 mm. Price 10 pence each.

No. 42 Police Set

1935–1940. Comprising:

42a Blue Police Box. Price 6 pence.

42b Blue and green motorcycle patrol, white rubber wheels. Price 10 pence.

42c Police officer directing traffic with white coat. Price 3 pence.

42d Police officer directing traffic with blue coat. Price 4 pence.

Price of set 1 shilling 11 pence.

No. 43 Royal Automobile Club Set

1935–1941. Comprising:

43a RAC Telephone Box. Price 6 pence.

43b RAC Motorcycle Patrol with white rubber tyres. Price 9 pence.

43c RAC guide directing traffic. Price 3 pence.

43d RAC guide at salute. Price 3 pence.

Price of complete set 1 shilling 9 pence.

No. 44 Automobile Association Set

1935–1941. Comprising:

44a AA Box complete with three signs. Price 8 pence.

44b AA Motorcycle Patrol. Price 9 pence.

44c AA Guide Directing Traffic. Price 3 pence.

44d AA Guide Saluting. Price 3 pence. With pictorial card stand.

Price of set 1 shilling 11 pence.

No. 47 Road Signs

1935–1954.

The twelve signs are:

1. 47e 30 MPH Limit.
2. 47f De-restriction.
3. 47g School.
4. 47h Steep Hill.
5. 47k S-Bend.
6. 47m Left-hand Bend.
7. 47n Right-hand Bend.
8. 47p T-Junction.
9. 47q No Entry.
10. 47r Major Road Ahead.
11. 47s Crossing No Gates.
12. 47t Roundabout.

Numbers 47i, 47j, 47l, 47o were omitted to avoid numeric confusion. Price 3 pence each. Price complete set 1 shilling 6 pence.

No. 49 Petrol Pumps (Renumbered 780 in 1950)

1935–1950. Comprising:

Pratt's Oil Bin and four Petrol Pumps with or without 'Pratt's' decals, with white (yellow) rubber hoses.

49a Bowser Petrol Pump, green.

49b Wayne Petrol Pump, turquoise.

49c Theo Petrol Pump, blue.

49d Shell Petrol Pump, red.

49e 'Pratt's' Oil Bin, deep yellow. Price 4 pence each except oil bin, 3 pence. Price for set 1 shilling 6 pence.

No. 050 Railway Staff

1961–1968. Comprising: twelve Dublo-scale figures in plastic, early sets with a Policeman, later sets with a Shunter. The set is in a clear compartmental Perspex case. Price of set 3 shillings.

No. 050 Ships of the Royal Navy

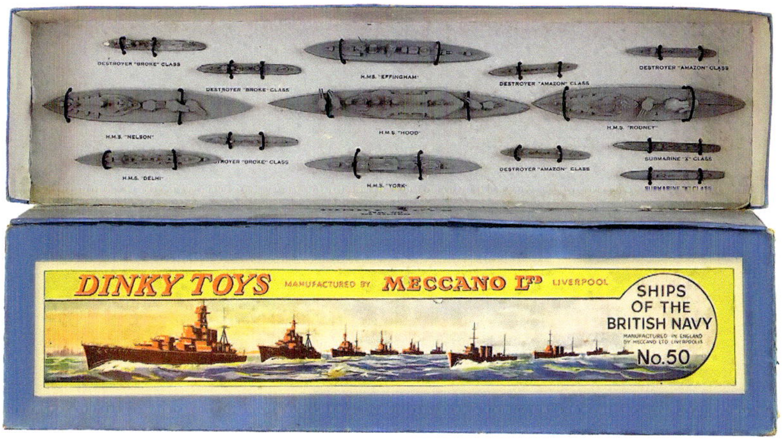

1934–1942. Comprising:

50a HMS *Hood*. Price 7 pence.

50b HMS *Nelson*. Price 6 pence.

50c HMS *Effingham*. Price 5 pence.

50d HMS *York*. Price 5 pence.

50e HMS *Delhi*. Price 4 pence.

Three 50f Broke Class Destroyers. Price 1½ pence each.

50g X Class Submarine. Price 1½ pence.

Three 50h Amazon Class Destroyers. Price 1½ pence each.

50k K Class Submarine. Price 1½ pence.

Price of set 3 shillings 6 pence.

No. 051 Station Staff

1954–1959. Comprising: six plastic station staff, 00 gauge.

Previously 1001 issued 1952 to 1954, then renumbered to 051. Price 2 shillings and 11 pence.

No. 51 Famous Liners

1934–1940. The famous British liners represented in this collection are the *Empress of Britain* in which King George V and Queen Mary returned from their Canadian tour, and the *Strathaird*, which is one of the largest vessels owned by the Peninsular and Oriental Steam Navigation Company. Other British vessels are *Queen of Bermuda*, owned by Furness, Withy and Co. Ltd, and the Cunard White Star *Britannic*. Two famous Continental liners are the Norddeutscher Lloyd *Europa* and the Italian liner *Rex*. Both of these have held for a time the Blue Riband of the Atlantic. Price of each was 7 pence. Price of complete set was 3 shillings and 6 pence.

No. 52 Railway Station Passengers

1961–1969. Comprising: eleven passenger figures and a bench. The set is in a clear compartmental Perspex case with backing card. Price of set 4 shillings 3 pence.

No. 053 Passengers

1954–1959. Comprising: six plastic passengers, 00 gauge.

Previously 1003 issued 1952 to 1954 then renumbered to 053. Price 2 shillings 3 pence.

Gentleman with Coat, Lady with Rug, Gentleman with Paper, Golfer, Lady Walking, Lady with Fur Coat.

No. 054 Railway Station Staff

1962–1970. Comprising: four station personnel and eight pieces of station accessories, including bicycle, suitcases and trolley. 00 gauge, plastic. The set is in a clear compartmental Perspex case with backing card. 1964 price of set 3 shillings 11 pence.

No. 60 British Aeroplanes Set Issue One

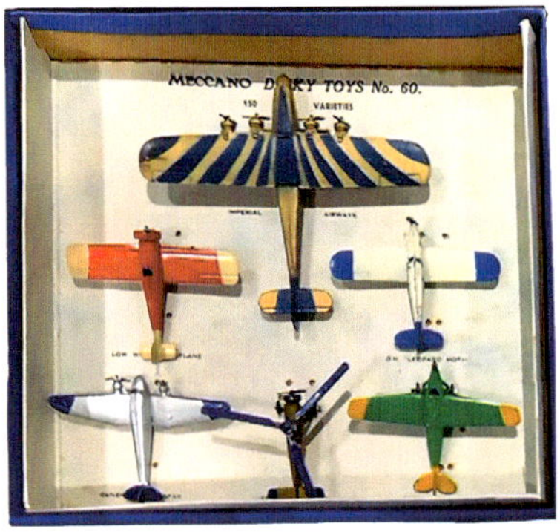

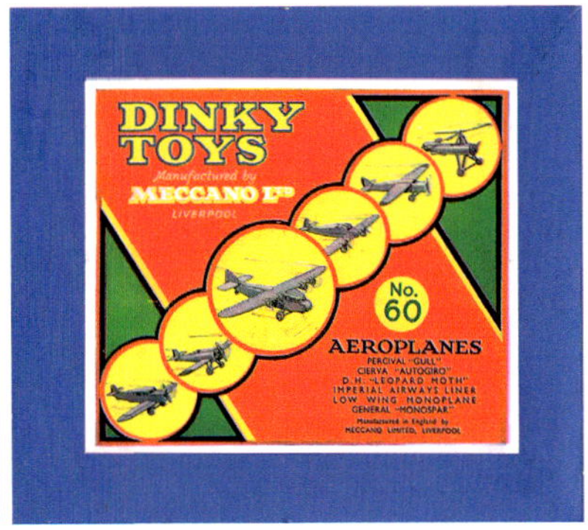

1934–1935. Aeroplanes set with no registration letters on aircraft wing comprising:

60a Imperial Airways Airliner, gold, blue striped markings to wing.

60b Leopard Moth, green, orange wing tips.

60c Percival Gull, white, blue wing tips.

60f Auto Giro, gold, blue wing tips and rotor.

60d Low Wing Monoplane, red, cream wing tips.

60e General Monospar, silver, blue wing tips.

60f Cierva Autogiro, gold and dark blue.

The set was reissued in 1936. Price of each 6 pence except 60a, 9 pence. Price of set 2 shillings.

No. 60 French Aeroplanes

1938–1939. Comprising:

60a Arc-en-Ciel in gold and blue with three two-blade propellers.

60b Potez 58 in yellow and grey with one two-bladed propeller.

60c Hanriot Type H180T in green and cream with one two-bladed propeller.

60d Breguet Type Corsaire in dark red and green with one two-bladed propeller.

60e Dewotine Type 500 in red and white with one two-bladed propeller.

60f Cierva Autogiro in gold and green with one green three-bladed rotor.

Price of set 3 shillings.

No. 60 British Aeroplanes Set Issue Two

1936–1941. Six aeroplanes with registration letters on the wings and wheeled undercarriages comprising:

60a Imperial Airways Liner with a gold body and the registration number G-ABTI. Price 9 pence.

60b DH Leopard Moth with a green body and the registration number G-ACPT. Price 6 pence.

60c Percival Gull with a white body and the registration number G-ADZO. Price 6 pence.

60d Low Wing Monoplane with a red body and the registration number G-AVYP. Price 6 pence.

60e General Monospar with a silver body and the registration number G-BAVP. Price 7 pence.

60f Cierva Autogiro Helicopter with a gold body with blue rotors and blue tail fin tips. Price 7 pence.

The individual aircraft were issued in 1934 and withdrawn in 1936. This complete set includes 'Gliding Game' instructions, a small envelope containing clips and a hank of blue string and was priced at 3 shillings.

No. 60a Imperial Airways Liner

No. 60b D.H. "Leopard Moth"

No. 60c Percival "Gull"

No. 60d Low Wing Monoplane

No. 60e General "Monospar"

No. 66f Army Co-operation Autogiro

No. 64 Aeroplane Set

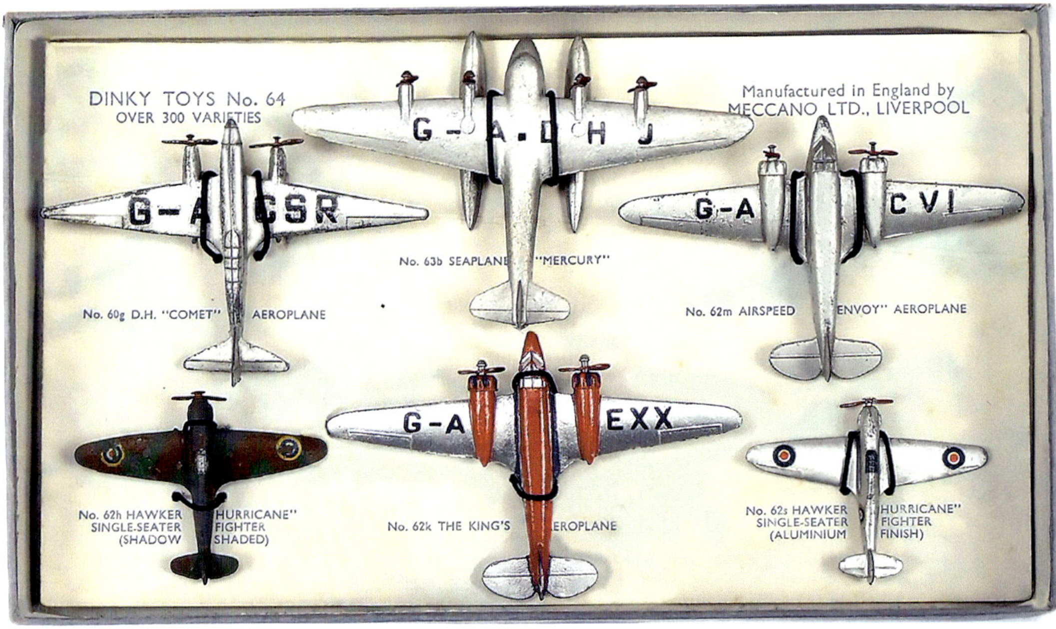

1939–1941. Comprising:

60g DH Comet, 1935 to 1941. Gold, wing marking G-ACSR. Advertised in *Meccano Magazine* in March 1936, priced 6 pence. Scale model of the aircraft used by Flying Officer A. E. Couston and Mrs Kirby-Green in their record-breaking flight from Croydon to Cape Town and back.

62h Hurricane, 1939 to 1941. In dark shaded camouflage, red and blue RAF roundels, wheels down, red and black underside. With or without landing gear. Advertised in *Meccano Magazine* in February 1939, priced 6 pence.

62k 'Kings Aeroplane', 1938 to 1941. Red, silver and blue, wing marking G-AEXX. Supplied to the air council for the King's Flight. Advertised in *Meccano Magazine* in May 1938, priced 8 pence.

62m Airspeed Envoy, 1938 to 1941. A twin-engine commercial monoplane, mid-blue, wing marking G-ADCA. Advertised in *Meccano Magazine* in May 1938, priced 6 pence.

62s Hurricane, 1939 to 1941. Aluminium silver colour, red and blue RAF roundels, wheels down. With or without landing gear. Advertised in *Meccano Magazine* in February 1939, priced 6 pence.

63b Mercury Sea Plane G-ADHJ, 1939 to 1941. Mail aircraft that was carried and launched in the air from 63a Flying Boat *Maia*. The model had a gliding game hole on top and a clamp underneath, for coupling with *Maia*. Advertised in *Meccano Magazine* in February 1939, priced 9 pence.

All models scale 1:192. Price of complete set 4 shillings.

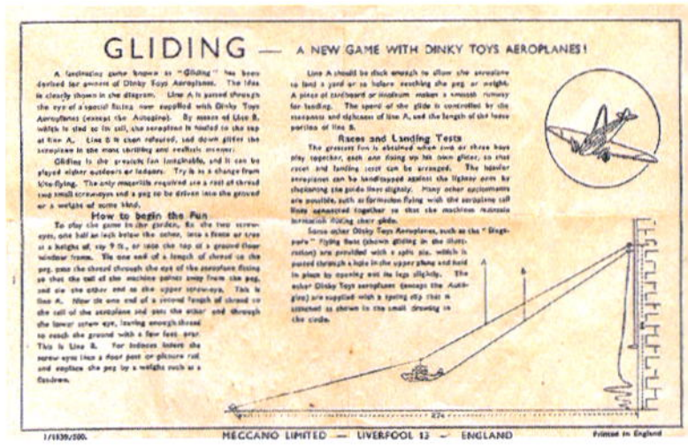

No. 65 Presentation Aeroplane Set

1939–1940. Comprising:

60r Empire Flying Boats of Imperial Airways were used in a fast air service between London and various parts of the Empire. They are four-engine, high-wing monoplanes with a maximum speed of nearly 200 mph. Price 1 shilling and 2 pence.

60t Douglas DC3 Airliner was one of the most popular types of air liner of the day. They were in regular use in the USA and also on some European routes. It was a twin-engined low-wing monoplane that could carry twenty-one passengers and had top speed of 213 mph. Price 11 pence.

60v Armstrong Whitworth Whitley Bomber was one of the newer type of bomber used by the Royal Air Force prior to the Second World War. It was a twin-engined middle-wing monoplane and was fitted with a retractable undercarriage. Price 11 pence.

60w Clipper III Flying Boat 'USA NC 16736' of Pan American Airlines took part in the 1937 transatlantic experimental flights between Newfoundland and Ireland which were carried out in cooperation with Imperial Airways. It is a Sikorsky S-42B flying boat. Price 1 shilling and 2 pence.

62n Junkers JU90, a scale model of what was at the time the latest German airliner. It was a four-engined monoplane in service with Lufthansa and carried forty-three passengers at a top speed of 256 mph. Price 1 shilling and 3 pence.

62p Armstrong Whitworth Ensign, this was the largest British airliner at the time. Six models were available with names Ensign, Elsinore, Explorer, Echo, Ettrick and Elysian. Price 1 shilling 3 pence.

62r De Havilland Albatross Mail Liner, scale model of one of the Albatross mail liners built for the Air Ministry for experimental flights. Price 1 shilling.

62w Imperial Airways Frobisher Class Airliner, built by the de Haviland Aircraft Company. They are four-engined low-wing monoplanes with a top speed of 225 mph. Three models were available: Frobisher, Falcon and Fortuna. Price 1 shilling.

All are finished in silver with red propellers, glide holes and hooks.

Price of set 8 shillings 6 pence.

No. 66 Camouflaged Aeroplanes Set

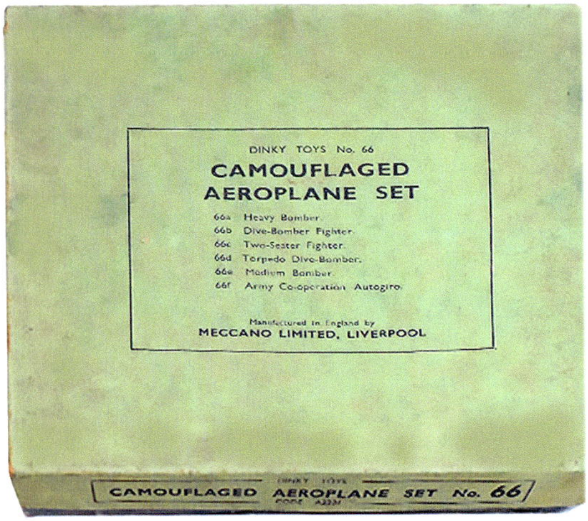

66a Heavy Bomber

66b Dive-Bomber Fighter

66c Two-Seater Fighter

66d Torpedo Dive-Bomber

66e Medium Bomber

66f Army Co-operation Autogiro

1940–1941. Comprising:

66a Heavy Bomber, 1940 to 1941. Reissue of 60a Imperial Airways Liner in Air Ministry shadow shading camouflage, blue and red RAF roundels, four double-blade silver tinplate propellers. Price 11 pence.

66b Dive Bomber Fighter, 1940 to 1941. Reissue of 60b Leopard Moth in shadow shading camouflage to upper surfaces and dark green to the underside, blue and red RAF roundels to upper wings. One silver tinplate single-blade propeller. Price 7 pence.

66c Two-seater Fighter, 1940 to 1941. Reissue of 60c Percival Gull in shadow shading camouflage, blue and red RAF roundels. One silver tinplate single-blade propeller. Price 7 pence.

66d Torpedo Dive Bomber, 1940 to 1941. Reissue of 60d Low Wing Monoplane in dark camouflage, red and blue RAF roundels. Price 8 pence.

66e Medium Bomber, 1940 to 1941. Reissue of 60e General Monospar in dark camouflage, red and blue RAF roundels. Price 9 pence.

66f Army Autogiro, 1940 to 1941. The Autogiro was finished in silver grey with red, white and blue RAF roundels, silver rotor blades and a red tinplate two-bladed propeller. Price 7 pence.

Packaged in a green card box with lift off lid. All models to scale 1:192. Price 10 shillings 6 pence.

No. 68 Aircraft in Service Set

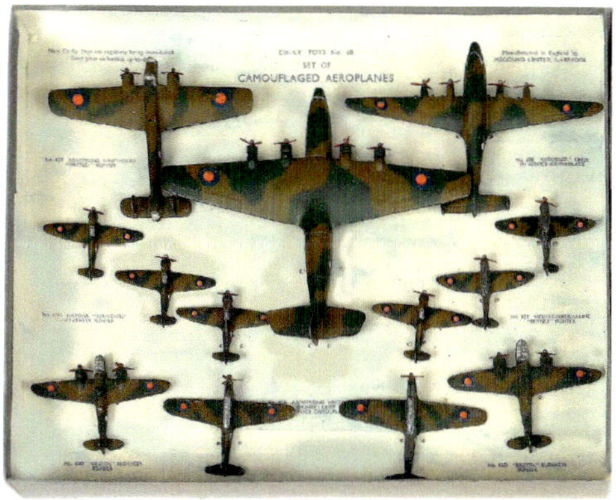

1940–1941. Comprising:

Two 60s Fairey Battle Bombers, two 62d Bristol Blenheim Bombers, three 62e Spitfires, three 62h Hawker Hurricanes, 62t Armstrong Whitworth Whitley Bomber, 68a Ensign Class Airliner and 68b Frobisher Class Airliner. All models in camouflage colours. First advertised in *Meccano Magazine* in July 1940. Price 10 shillings 6 pence. Scale of all models 1:192.

No. 101 Dining Room Furniture Set

1936–1940. Comprising:

101a Table. Price 4 pence.

101b Sideboard with opening doors. Price 7 pence.

101c Carver Chairs, two in number. Price 2½ pence each.

101d Chairs, four in number. Price 1½ pence each.

Supplied in walnut brown finish only. Price of set 1 shilling 9 pence.

No. 102 Bedroom Furniture Set

1936–1940. Comprising:

102a Bed. Price 5 pence. 102b Wardrobe with opening doors. Price 7 pence. 102c Dressing Table with opening drawers. Price 5 pence. 102d Dressing Chest with opening drawer. Price 8 pence. 102e Dressing Table Stool. Price 1½ pence. 102f Chair. Price 1½ pence. Supplied in walnut brown finish or two colour schemes of mauve and gold or dark green and light green. Price of set 2 shillings 3 pence.

No. 103 Kitchen Furniture Set

1936–1940. Comprising:

103a Refrigerator with opening door. Price 6½ pence. 103b Kitchen Cabinet with opening door. Price 8 pence. 103c Electric Cooker with opening drawers. Price 5 pence. 103d Table. Price 3½ pence. 103e Chair. Price 1½ pence. Supplied in two colour schemes of light blue and white and light green and cream. Price of set 2 shillings.

No. 104 Bathroom Furniture Set

1936–1940. Comprising:

104a Bath. Price 4½ pence. 104b Bath Mat. Price ½ pence. 104c Pedestal Hand Basin. Price 4½ pence. 104d Stool. Price 1½ pence. 104e Linen Basket with hinged lid. Price 3 pence. 104f Toilet with hinged lid. Price 4½ pence. Supplied in a two-colour schemes of pink and white or light green and white. Price of set 1 shilling 6 pence.

No. 118 Tow-away Glider Set

1965–1969. Comprising:

135 Triumph 2000, white with mid-blue roof, red interior, opening boot and bonnet, luggage, fingertip steering, suspension. White glider trailer with drop-down tailboard. Red and yellow glider with removable transparent canopy. Length 286 mm. Price 14 shillings 11 pence.

No. 121 Goodwood Sports Cars

1963–1966. Comprising:

112 Austin Healey Sprite Mark II, introduced 1961, red body, fingertip steering, four-wheel suspension, detailed dashboard, driver, plastic windscreen. Length 78 mm. Price 4 shillings.

113 MGB, introduced in 1962, cream body, fingertip steering, driver, opening doors, plastic windscreen. Length 85 mm. Price 5 shillings 9 pence.

120 Jaguar E-type introduced in 1962, red body, black interchangeable hood. It has fingertip steering, driver, plastic windscreen, detailed baseplate. Length 91 mm. Price 6 shillings.

182 Porsche 356. Introduced in 1958, cream (blue) body. Length 87 mm. Price 2 shillings 11 pence.

Also includes nine plastic figures. Price of set 27 shillings 11 pence.

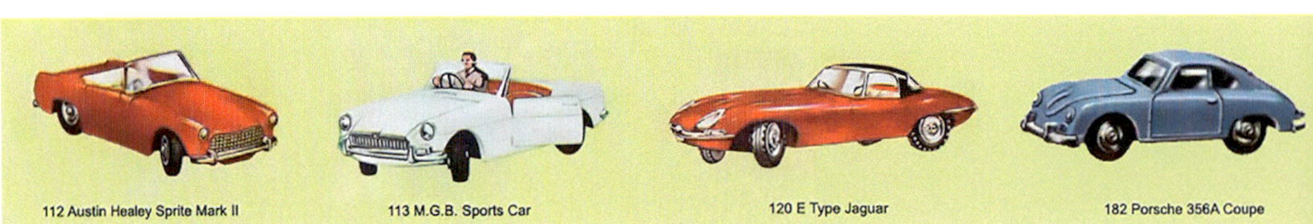

No. 122 Touring

1963–1965. Comprising:

188 Caravan, introduced in 1961, cream and blue (cream and green) body. Independent suspension, detailed interior fittings including a table and draining board. It has an opening door and glazed windows. A towing hook allows it to be towed by any Dinky passenger car. Length 132 mm. Price 5 shillings 6 pence.

193 Station Wagon, introduced in 1961, yellow and white body. Independent suspension, steering wheel, fingertip steering, luggage rack, chromed bumpers and radiator. Length 102 mm. Price 6 shillings 3 pence.

195 Jaguar, introduced in 1960, yellow and white body. It has four-wheel suspension, steering wheel, fingertip steering. Length 95 mm. Price 3 shillings 11 pence.

270 'AA' Patrol Motorcycle and Sidecar, introduced in 1959, yellow body with an AA badge on the sidecar and driver. Length 46 mm. Renumbered from 44b. The 1959 price 2 shillings 2 pence.

295 Atlas Kenebrake Bus, introduced in 1960, light blue and grey body, four-wheel suspension, steering wheel, windows, seat. Length 86 mm. Renumbered from 44b. Price 3 shillings 9 pence.

796 Healey Sports Boat on Trailer, introduced in 1960, bright green decking and cream hull and is on an orange trailer from which it is detachable. The boat is constructed in plastic and floats. It has a steering wheel and windscreen. Price 3 shillings 3 pence.

Price of set 35 shillings 11 pence.

No. 123 Mayfair

1963–1965. Comprising:

142 Jaguar Mk.10, introduced in 1962, metallic blue body. Independent suspension, steering wheel, fingertip steering, windows, interior fittings, a boot that opens, luggage. Length 106 mm. Price 5 shillings 6 pence.

150 Rolls-Royce Silver Wraith, introduced in 1962 in two-tone grey body. Independent suspension, windows, steering wheel. Length 117 mm. Price 5 shillings 6 pence.

186 Mercedes Benz 220 SE, introduced in 1961, blue body, independent suspension, windows, left-hand-drive steering wheel, fingertip steering, interior fittings. Length 102 mm. Price 5 shillings 9 pence.

194 Bentley S Series Coupé, introduced in 1961, bronze (grey, cream) body, independent suspension, windows, left-hand-drive steering wheel, fingertip steering, interior fittings. Length 112 mm. Price 6 shillings 3 pence.

198 Rolls Royce Phantom V, introduced in 1962, two-tone green and cream body, independent suspension, opening windows, steering wheel, fingertip steering, interior fittings, driver. Length 112 mm. Price 6 shillings 11 pence.

199 Austin 7 Countryman, introduced in 1961, pale blue body, independent suspension, windows, fingertip steering, interior fittings. Length 72 mm. Price 3 shillings 6 pence.

All the models came with spun hubs and the set included one female and three male figures. Price of set 35 shillings 11 pence.

No. 124 Holidays

1964–1966. Comprising:

952 Vega Luxury Coach, grey and maroon body. Length 242 mm. Price 21 shillings. 137 Plymouth Fury, grey (green, blue) body. Length 122 mm. Price 5 shillings 11 pence. Price of set 35 shillings 11 pence.

No. 125 Fun A'Hoy Set

1964–1966. Comprising:

130 Ford Consul Corsair with a blue(red) body. Length 106 mm. Price 5 shillings 11 pence. 796 Healey Sports Boat on Trailer (described page 55).

No. 126 Motor Show Presentation Set

1967–1968. Comprising:

127 Rolls-Royce Silver Cloud III, gold body, chrome spun wheels, jewelled lights. Issued in 1965 with a metallic green body. Price 9 shillings 11 pence. Length 124 mm. Registration number plate FTR 476.

133 Cortina, yellow (dark yellow) body (white roof), spun wheels, jewelled lights, red interior. Issued in 1964 in gold with a white roof. Price 6 shillings and 11 pence. Length 101 mm. Registration number plate MTB 217C.

151 Vauxhall Victor 101, metallic lemon body, red interior, spun wheels, jewelled lights, chrome window surround. Issued in 1965 in gold with opening boot and bonnet, price of 7 shillings 11 pence. Length 102 mm. Registration number plate INJ 483C.

171 Austin 1800, metallic blue, spun wheels, jewelled lights, chrome window surround, red interior, chrome hubs. Issued in 1965 in gold with opening boot and bonnet. Price 7 shillings 11 pence. Length 100 mm. Registration number plate UVR 567B.

Housed in a presentation plastic window yellow card box. Price of set 31 shillings 6 pence.

No.127 Rolls Royce Silver Cloud III

No.133 Cortina

No.151 Vauxhall Victor 101

No.171 Austin 1800

No. 149 Sports Cars

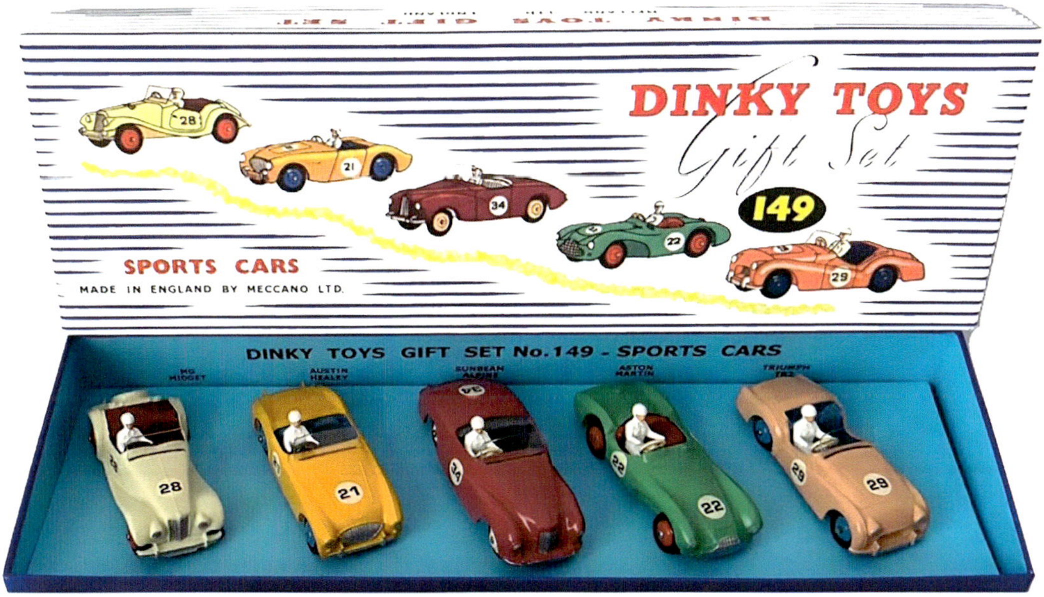

1958–1961. Comprising:

107 Sunbeam Alpine, cerise with cream ridged hubs, silver trim, pale grey interior, bright axles, bright baseplate and intact windscreen. Racing number 34. Length 94 mm. Price 3 shillings 11 pence.

108 MG Midget, white with red ridged hubs, silver trim, maroon interior, slight tarnishing to axles, bright baseplate and intact windscreen. Racing number 28. Length 83 mm. Price 3 shillings 9 pence.

109 Austin-Healey comes in deep yellow with mid-blue ridged hubs, silver trim, mid-blue interior. Racing number 21, Length 85 mm. Price 3 shillings 9 pence.

110 Aston Martin DB3S, mid-green with red ridged hubs, silver trim, red interior. Racing number 22. Length 87 mm. Price 3 shillings 6 pence.

111 Triumph TR2, pink with mid-blue ridged hubs, silver trim, mid-blue interior. Racing number 29. Length 84 mm. Price 3 shillings 6 pence.

Price of set 15 shillings.

No. 150 Royal Armoured Corp Personnel Pre-war

1937–1941. Comprising:

150a Officer, 150b two seated Privates, 150c two standing Privates, 150b Non Commissioned Officer, all are black except No. 150a in khaki. Came in a blue box. Price each 3 pence. Price of set 1 shilling 6 pence.

No. 150 Royal Armoured Corp Personnel Post-war

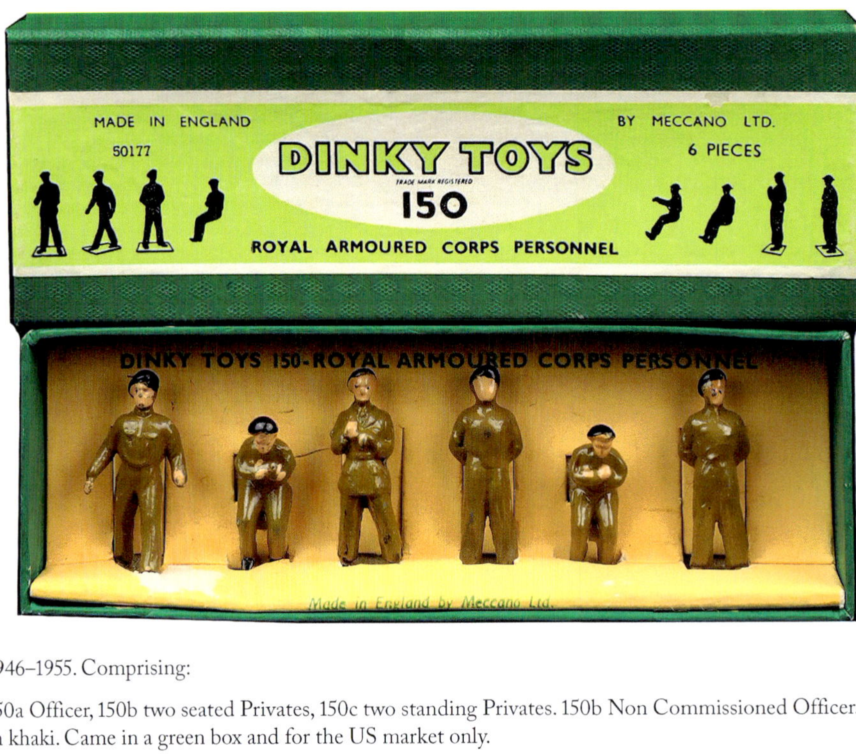

1946–1955. Comprising:

150a Officer, 150b two seated Privates, 150c two standing Privates. 150b Non Commissioned Officer. All were in khaki. Came in a green box and for the US market only.

No. 151 RTC Medium Tanks Set

1937–1940. Comprising:

151A Medium Tank, issued December 1937 to 1940. Length 92 mm. Gloss green with white squadron markings. Rotating turret with aerial and bright wire chain tracks. Price 1 shilling 6 pence. Also reissued for the US market only between 1945 and 1953 in matt green with no triangle and black wire chain tracks.

151B then 620 Transport 6 Wheel Lorry. Issued 1937 to 1941 and also released post-war between 1946 and 1954. Length 99 mm. Price 1 shilling. Pre-war models were in gloss or matt green paint but post-war also in US army drab brown. Pre-war the model had thin axles with crimped ends and smooth wheels. Post-war it had thick axles with smooth wheels and then later with ridged ones.

151C Cooker Trailer. Issued 1937 to 1941 and reissued in 1946 to 1948. Length 60 mm. Price 6 pence. *Meccano Magazine* of February 1938 describes the cooker trailer as a mobile canteen with a fire fed by petrol under pressure which is capable of doing the cooking for the whole battalion.

151D Water Tank Trailer, issued 1937 to 1941 and reissued 1946 to 1948. Length 52 mm. Price 5 pence. Gloss green. *Meccano Magazine* of February 1938 describes the water tank trailer as having a capacity of 300 gallons with a filter tank, a purification cylinder and three taps.

Sold in a lift-off-lid box with fold-down flap. The set was advertised in *Meccano Magazine* in October 1937 with an issue price of 3 shillings 9 pence. All to a scale 1:59.

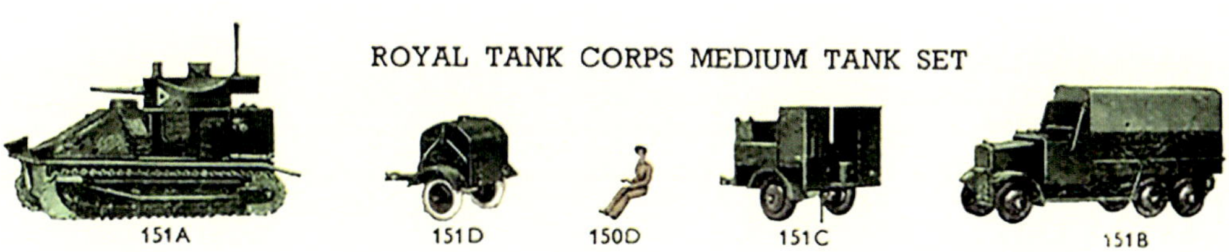

No. 152 RTC Light Tank Set

1937–1941. Comprising:

152A Light Tank. Issued November 1937 to 1940 and reissued 1947 to 1954. Length 68 mm. Matt or gloss green or in brown with rotating turret and aerial. White RTC triangle squadron markings and chain tracks. Early post-war with green base and then later in black. No triangle post-war fairly common in green. Brown USA army version rare. Price 1 shilling and then 2 shillings 11 pence on reissue.

152B and 152/B2 then 671 Reconnaissance Car. Issued November 1937 to 1940. Reissued in 1946 to 1954. Length 89 mm. Military green with six wheels. Pre-war the model had thin axles and post-war thick ones. Smooth and then later ridged tyres. Black or green baseplate with green body. Second version with black baseplate with US brown body. Green version common and US military brown rare. Price 1 shilling and then 2 shillings 11 pence on reissue.

152C Austin 7 Military Car. Issued November 1937 to 1941. Length 51 mm. Pre-war only. Army Driver 150d had to be purchased separately. The model is based on the Austin 7 PD Type Military Tourer which with a combination of light weight and high manoeuvrability meant that it could often tackle rough ground that would leave a larger, more powerful vehicle floundering on its axles.

The set was advertised in *Meccano Magazine* in October 1937 with an issue price of 3 shillings 9 pence. Could be bought as a set or individual models. All to scale 1:59.

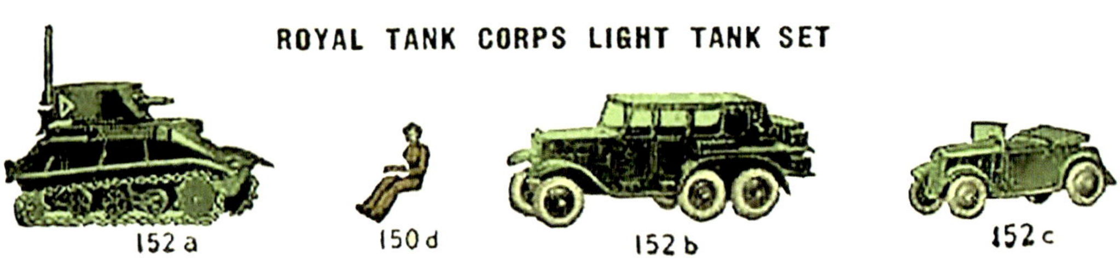

No. 156 Mechanised Army Set

1939–1940. This was the ultimate in pre-war military sets and contained 151A, 151B, 151C, 151D, 152A, 152B, 152C, as previously described in Sets 151 and 152 plus 161A, 161B, 162A, 162B and 162C which are described below.

161A Searchlight on Lorry. Issued March 1939 to 1941. In gloss or matt green paint. Thin axles with crimped ends. Smooth wheels. Length 99 mm. Price 1 shilling 6 pence.

161B AA Gun on Trailer. Issued March 1939 to 1941. Matt green or brown. Gun elevates and swivels. Folding sides and holes in seats for gunners. Tow-bar and hook. Pre-war with open baseplate and 0.062-inch axles. Early smooth wheels and later ridged. Common in green but rare in US army brown. Length 115 mm. Price 1 shilling 6 pence.

162A Light Dragon Motor Tractor. Issued March 1939 to 1941. Green with green or black baseplate. Other versions included camouflaged colours and US army green for an export model. Chain tracks with bright or black chains but some models have rubber wheels instead of chains. There are model versions with none or four or five holes in the seats for the men. Length 89 mm. Price 1 shilling 3 pence.

162B Ammunition Trailer. Issued March 1939 to 1941. With smooth wheels and 0.062-inch axles with green baseplate. This trailer (or 'Limber') fits between the Light Dragon Tractor and the 18-Pounder Field Gun. Length 54 mm. Price 5 pence.

162C 18-Pounder Gun. Issued March 1939 to 1941. Smooth wheels and 0.062-inch axles with pre-war green baseplate. Length 78 mm. Price 5 pence.

All to scale 1:59. Price of set 12 shillings 6 pence.

161A 161B 162C 162B 162A

No. 160 Royal Artillery Personnel (Yellow Box)

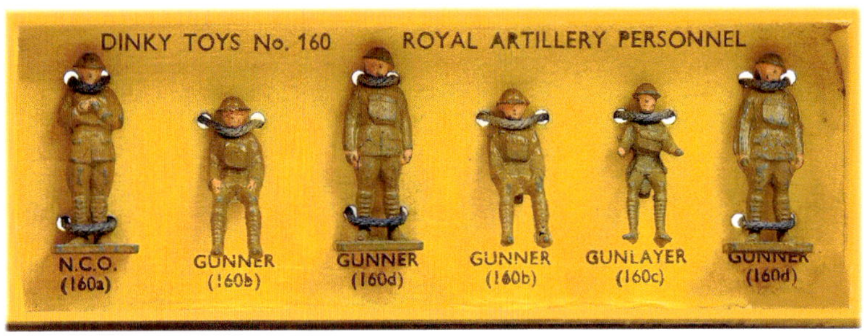

1939–1940 and reissued 1951 to 1954, then number changed to 606. Set contains 160a NCO, 160b Gunner seated, 160c Gunner seated with arms out and 160d Gunner standing. All dressed in khaki. Post-war export only. Advertised in *Meccano Magazine* in September 1939 with an issue price of 10 pence for the set or individual prices of 2 pence for the NCO and 1½ pence for the other models.

No. 160, then 606 Royal Artillery Personnel (Green Box)

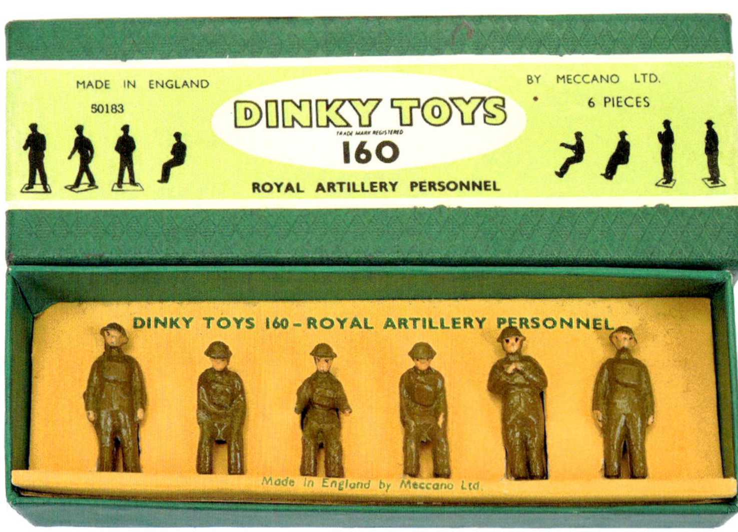

Contained the same figures as those in the yellow box sold in the UK but re-boxed in the green box and issued for US export only between 1952 and 1954 before the number was changed to 606 in 1954. This was a new die casting as the figures in the pre-war 160 set had puttees around their leg and in this issue are wearing fatigues without them.

No. 161 Mobile Anti-Aircraft Unit

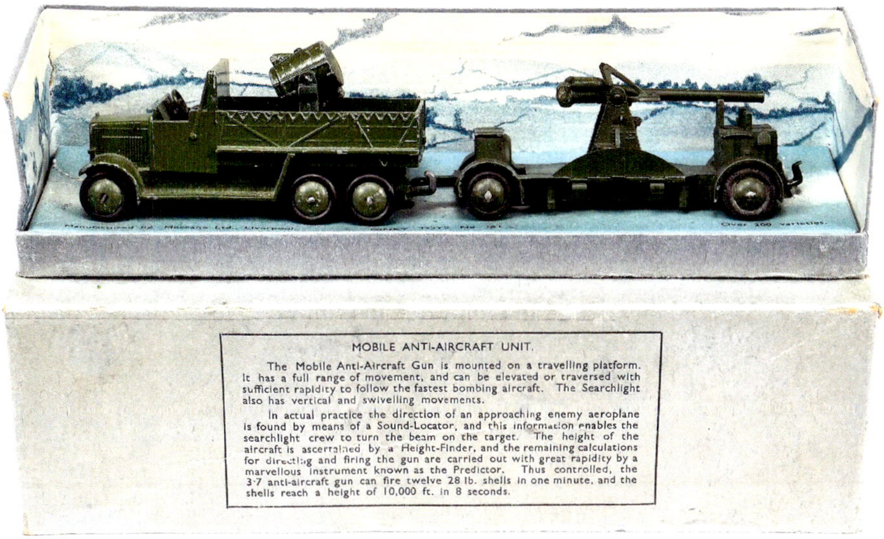

1939–1941. Comprising:

161a Searchlight on a lorry. Length 99 mm. Price 1 shilling 6 pence.

161b AA Gun on a Trailer. Length 115 mm. Price 1 shilling 6 pence. The gun and searchlight on the model can be elevated and swivelled and the sides of the gun platform can be folded down. The models have holes in seats for use with the figures in the 160 Royal Artillery Personal set. Scale 1:59. Price of set 3 shillings.

No. 162, then 691, 18-Pounder Quick-firing Field Gun Set

1938–1941. Comprising:

162a Light Dragon Motor Tractor. Issued March 1939 to 1941. Length 89 mm. Price 1 shilling 3 pence.

162b Ammunition Trailer. Issued March 1939 to1 941. Length 54 mm. Price 5 pence.

162c 18-Pounder Gun. Issued March 1939 to 1941. Length 78 mm. Price 5 pence. Price of set 2 shillings. Scale 1:59. Reissued 1946 to 1948.

No. 201 Racing Cars

1965–1968. Comprising:

240 Cooper Racing Car, mid-blue body, racing number 20, side labels, and bonnet decal. Length 80 mm.

241 Lotus Racing Car, mid-green body, driver, racing number 24, side labels, bonnet decal. Length 80 mm.

242 Ferrari F1 Racing Car, red body, racing number 36, side labels, bonnet decal. Length 89 mm.

243 BRM Racing Car, metallic green body, yellow plastic engine cover, racing number 7, side labels, bonnet decal. Length 82 mm.

All four racing cars have removable cowlings to show the engine, spun hubs, driver, plastic windscreen and independent suspension. Set includes four figures. Price 3 shillings 11 pence each. Price of set 21 shillings.

No.240 Cooper Racing Car

No.241 Lotus Racing Car

No.242 Ferrari F1 Racing Car

No.243 BRM Racing Car

No. 237 Dinky Way Set

1978–1979. Export version of set 240. Comprising:

Model Roadway System, twenty Traffic Signs. Vehicles include 410 Bedford Van, no decals. Length 90 mm. 211 Triumph TR77. Length 98 mm. 183 Morris Mini Minor. Length 90 mm. 382 Dumper Truck. Length 118 mm. Printed for right-hand driving.

No. 240 Dinky Way Set

1978–1980. Comprising:

211 Triumph TR7, red. Length 98 mm. 255 Police Mini, pale blue and white. Length 82 mm. 382 Convoy Series Dump Truck, red and grey. Length 118 mm. 412 Bedford AA Van, yellow. Length 90 mm. Model Roadway System, twenty Road Signs, two sets of traffic lights, decals and instructions. Left-hand driving. Price of set 8 pounds 95 pence.

No. 245 Superfast Set

1969–1973. Comprising:

131 E-Type Jaguar, 1968 to 1977, white, red detailed interior, plated wing mirrors, number plates front and rear. Finely spoked silver cast wheels. Silver plastic aerial. Opening doors, bonnet with a detailed silver engine, side-opening rear hatch. Length 112 mm. 1969 price 13 shillings 11 pence.

153 Aston Martin DB6, 1967 to 1971. Silver-blue metallic finish, red interior, spoked wheels, number plates at both ends. Opening doors, bonnet, detailed silver engine, opening rear hatch. Length 111 mm. 1969 price 11 shillings 11 pence.

188 Jensen FF, 1968, yellow finish, detailed black interior, cast wheels. Opening bonnet and doors, jewelled lights. Front and rear number plates. Length 121 mm. 1969 price 10 shillings 9 pence.

A superfast wheels set. Price 38 shillings 11 pence.

No. 246 International GT Set

1969–1973. Comprising:

216 Dino Ferrari, blue, 1967 to 1974, white wide-opening bonnet, opening doors, detailed interior, number 20. Length 98 mm. 1969 Price 10 shillings and 6 pence.

187 De Tomaso Mangusta, 1968 to 1976, fluorescent pink and white, gull wing, rear engine model with lift-up see-through covers, opening doors, luggage goes under the bonnet, number 1. Length 102 mm. 1969 price 10 shillings and 9 pence, number 1.

215 Ford GT Racing Car, 1965 to 1973, metallic green opening engine cover and bonnet, wrap-around windscreen, steering wheel and seats and opening doors, competition number 7. Length 96 mm. 1969 price 8 shillings and 11 pence.

Price of set 32 shillings 6 pence.

No. 249 World-famous Racing Cars

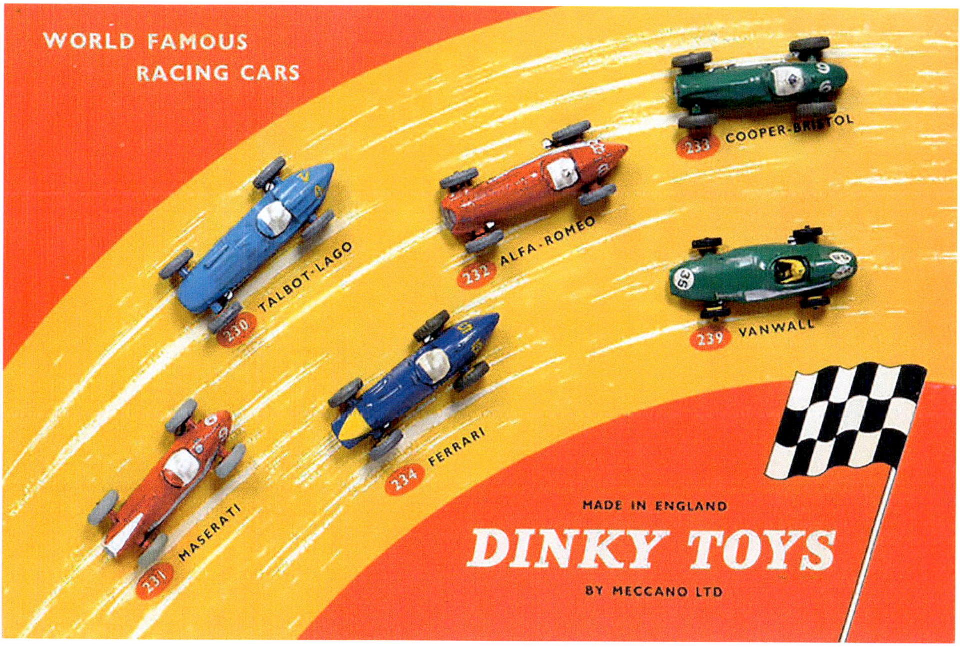

1962–1963. Comprising the following six models, four of which previously included in the 4 (renumbered 243) Racing Cars Set:

230 Talbot Lago, introduced in 1954, light blue body, cast in driver. Racing number 4. Length 103 mm. 1962 price 3 shillings 3 pence. Renumbered from 23k.

231 Maserati, introduced in 1954, red body with a white flash down the side and on the nose, cast in driver. Racing number 9. Length 94 mm. 1962 price 3 shillings 3 pence. Renumbered from 23n.

232 Alfa Romeo, introduced in 1954, light blue body, cast in driver. Racing number 8. Length 100 mm. 1962 price 3 shillings 3 pence. Renumbered from 23p.

233 Cooper Bristol, introduced in 1954, green body with a yellow nose, cast in driver. Racing number 6. Length 189 mm. 1962 price 3 shillings 3 pence. Renumbered from 23g.

234 Ferrari, introduced in 1954, light blue body, cast in driver. Racing number 6. Length 101 mm. 1962 price 3 shillings 3 pence. Renumbered from 23h.

239 Vanwall, introduced in 1958, light blue body with Vanwall written on the side and has a steering wheel and a separate driver. Racing number 35. Length 95 mm. 1962 price 3 shillings 6 pence. Renumbered from 23k.

Price of set 1 pound 2 shillings.

No. 280 Delivery Vans (see also 28)

1939–1940. Type 3 casting comprising: 280a 'Viyella' van, 280b 'Hartley's' van, 280c 'Shredded Wheat' van, 280d 'Bisto' van, 280e 'Yorkshire Evening Post' van and 280f 'Mackintosh's' van. Individually priced at 6 pence each, complete set sold for 3 shillings.

No. 294 Police Vehicles

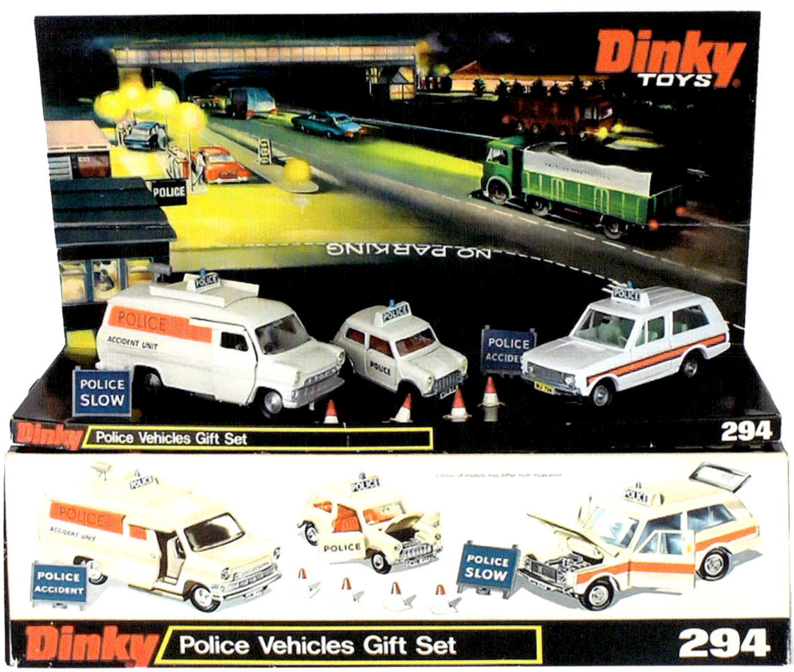

1973–1977. Comprising: 250 Mini Cooper S. Length 75 mm. Price 50 pence. 254 Police Range Rover. Length 109 mm. Price 85 pence. 287 Ford Transit Accident Unit. Length 122 mm. Price 1 pound 15 pence. With a policeman figure, four traffic cones and two road signs. Price of set 2 pounds 90 pence.

No. 298 Emergency Services

1963–1966. Comprising:

258 Ford Fairlane US Police Car with policeman figure. Length 116 mm. Price 4 shillings 11 pence.

263 Superior Criterion Ambulance with stretcher and female attendant. Length 127 mm. Price 7 shillings 11 pence.

277 Superior Criterion Ambulance with roof beacon and male attendant. Length 127 mm. Price 8 shillings 11 pence.

276 'Airport Fire Control' Fire Engine. Length 117 mm. Price 9 shillings 11 pence.

Price of set 35 shillings 11 pence.

No. 299/1 Post Office Services

1957–1959. Comprising:

260 Morris Commercial Royal Mail Van. Length 78 mm. Price 3 shillings.

261 Post Office Telephone Service Van. Length 73 mm. Price 3 shilling 3 pence.

750 Telephone Kiosk. Height 66 mm. Price 1 shilling 3 pence.

011 Telegraph Messenger. Height 35 mm. Price 9 pence.

012 Postman. Height 35 mm. Price 9 pence.

No. 299/2 Motorway Services

1963–1966. Comprising:

434 Bedford Crash Truck. Length 123 mm. Price 7 shillings 11 pence.

269 Motorway Police Car. Length 97 mm. Price 4 shillings 11 pence.

257 Fire Chief's Car. Length 102 mm. Price 3 shillings 11 pence.

276 Airport Fire Tender. Length 117 mm. Price 9 shillings 11 pence.

277 Superior Criterion Ambulance. Length 127 mm. Price 8 shillings 11 pence.

Price of set 35 shillings 11 pence.

No. 299 Crash Squad Set

1978–1979. Comprising:

732 Bell Police Helicopter, clear bubble-type cockpit canopy, rotating main and tail rotors, simulated engine detail, pilot. Length 211 mm. Price 1 pound 75 pence.

244 Plymouth Fury police car. Length 161 mm. Price 1 pound 65 pence The set comes with separate police road sign boards and traffic cones. Scale 1:60.

Price of set 3 pounds 49 pence.

No. 300 London Scene

1978–1979. Comprising:

289 Routemaster Bus, red exterior, pale blue interior, windows, seats, destination boards, adverts, speedwheels. Length 121 mm. 1979 price 1 pound 85 pence.

284 London Taxi, black, cast wheels, driver, windows, interior seat moulding. Length 112 mm. 1979 price 1 pound 99 pence.

No. 303 Commando Squad

1978–1980. Comprising:

687 Convoy Army Truck. Length 110 mm. 1979 price 1 pound 20 pence.

667 Armoured Car. Length 80 mm. 1979 price 1 pound 35 pence.

732 Bell Army Helicopter. Repainted Police Helicopter only issued with this set. Length 211 mm. All military green with black plastic wheels, camouflage net. Scale 1:48.

Later renamed as the Combat Arm set. 1979 price of set 3 pounds 99 pence.

No. 304 Fire Rescue

1978–1979. Comprising:

282 Land Rover Fire Appliance. Removable ladder, opening doors, glazed window. Length 119 mm. 1979 price 2 pounds 99 pence.

384 Fire Rescue Truck. Windows, seat, elevating swivelling snorkel arm topped by a hinged fire-fighting platform. Length 126 mm. 1979 price 1 pound 99 pence.

195 Fire Chief's Range Rover car. Opening doors, bonnet and tailgate, engine representation, glazed windows, detailed interior. Length 109 mm. 1977 price 1 pound 99 pence.

1979 Price of set 4 pounds 99 pence.

No. 307 Avengers Set

This set was planned originally for 1979 and was featured in the 1978–1979 Dinky Meccano catalogue. Sadly the set was never issued due to industrial action and the closing of the Binns Road factory in 1979. Only a small number of pre-production models were made. These are very rare and very expensive.

No. 309 Star Trek

1978–1980. Comprising:

358 USS Enterprise from the science fiction series Star Trek. Length 234 mm. 1979 price 3 pounds 25 pence.

357 Klingon Battlecruiser complete with pod and missiles. Length 228 mm. 1979 price 3 pounds 25 pence.

1979 price of set 7 pounds 45 pence.

No. 370 Dragster Set

1969–1974. Comprising:

A yellow and red dragster car with a white (blue, red) spring-launcher unit. First issue in cardboard box and then in a bubble box. Length 113 mm. 1971 price 99 pence.

No. 398 Farm Equipment

1964–1965. Farm set renumbered from set 1 but without the Moto-Kart and including the Hay Rake. Comprising:

300 Massey Ferguson Tractor. Red body, blue plastic driver, yellow hubs (metal to rear plastic to front). Length 89 mm. 1964 price 4 shillings 11 pence.

320 Harvest Trailer. Red ,yellow plastic hubs. Length 133 mm. 1964 price 4 shillings 11 pence.

321 Manure Spreader. Red, silver, yellow plastic hubs. Length 121 mm. 1964 price 4 shillings 11 pence.

322 Disc Harrow. Red and yellow. Length 86 mm. 1964 price 2 shillings 11 pence.

324 Hay Rake. Red, yellow cast wheels, Length 76 mm.1964 price 3 shillings 11 pence.

1964 price of set 21 shillings.

No. 399 Farm Tractor and Trailer

1970–1971. Comprising:

300 Massey Ferguson Tractor, red, yellow metal and plastic wheels, chimney, blue plastic driver. Length 89 mm. 1971 price 0.35 pounds.

428 Trailer, red grey chassis, steel wheels. Length 111 mm. 1971 price 35 pence.

1971 price of set 79 pence.

No. 399 Convoy Trucks

1977–1979. Comprising:

380 Skip Truck. Working skip-loading mechanism, removable skip which can be swung on and off the vehicle. Length 112 mm.

381 Farm Truck. High-sided, slatted load body, drop-down loading ramp. Length 110 mm.

382 Dumper Truck. Tipping high-capacity load body. Length 118 mm.

The cab and chassis unit on all three models is fitted with windows, seats and headlamps. 1979 price 1 pound 20 pence each. 1979 price of set 3 pounds 49 pence.

No. 600, previously 150, Armoured Corps Personnel

A post-war release of the old RTC set number 150 issued for USA export only between 1952 and 1954 before the number was changed to 600 in 1954. Scale 1:59. All figures in khaki only.

No. 606, previously 160, Royal Artillery Personnel

A post-war release of the old 160 Royal Artillery Personnel set issued for USA export only between 1952 and 1954 before the number was changed to 606 in 1954. Scale 1:59. All figures in khaki only.

No. 615 US Jeep with 105 mm Howitzer

1967–1978. Comprising:

Jeep. Green, authentic US markings, windscreen, driver. Length 108 mm. 105 mm Howitzer. Green, fires plastic shells. Length 199 mm. Set contains camouflage netting. Reviewed in *Meccano Magazine* in January 1968. Price 18 shillings 11 pence. Scale 1:32.

No. 616 AEC Artic Transporter with Chieftain Tank

1976–1978. Comprising:

Artic Transporter with AEC cab. Glazed windows, drop-down ramps, bogie wheels. Scale 1:42.

Chieftain Tank. Rotating turret with an elevating gun, fires plastic shells. Scale 1:50. Overall Length with ramps down is 318 mm.

Price of set 1 pound 1 shilling.

No. 617 Volkswagen KDF and 50 mm P.A.K. Anti-Tank Gun

1968–1978. Comprising: Volkswagen KDF. Length 115 mm. Dark greyish-green German army colour. German cross on each side. 625 – a 50 mm P.A.K. Anti-Tank Gun. Fires plastic shells. Length 159 mm. Reviewed in *Meccano Magazine* in January 1968. Price 16 shillings 11 pence. Scale 1:32.

No. 618 AEC Artic Transporter with Helicopter

1976–1978. Comprising:

Artic Transporter with AEC cab. Glazed windows, drop-down ramps, bogie wheels. Scale 1:42. Length with ramps down 318 mm.

Helicopter. Army version of model 736 Bundesmarine Sea King. Rotating blades, opening side door, lifting winch. Scale 1:103.

The set contains a camouflage net. Price of set 1 pound 25 pence.

No. 619 Bren Gun Carrier with Anti-Tank Gun

1976–1977. Comprising:

622 Bren Gun Carrier. Two figures, US markings. Length 125 mm. 1977 price 1 pound 99 pence.

625 Anti-Tank Gun. Fires plastic shells. Length 159 mm. 1977 price 1 pound 25 pence. 1977 price of set 2 pound 99 pence. Scale 1:32.

No. 677 Task Force Set

1972–1975. Comprising:

680 Ferret Armoured Car. Length 80 mm. 1973 price 30 pence. Scale 1:48.

681 DUKW. Length 127 mm. 1973 price 35 pence. Scale 1:76.

682 Stalwart Load. Carrier. Length 132 mm. 1973 price 30 pence. Scale 1:55.

Packaged in a card plinth display box. 1973 price of set 95 pence.

No. 691, Previously 162, Field Gun Unit

1952–1954. For the US export market only. Scale 1:59. Set contains 162a Light Dragon Motor Tractor, 162b Ammunition Trailer and 162c, the 18-Pounder Gun.

No. 695 Howitzer and Tractor Set

1962–1965. Comprising:

689 Medium Artillery Tractor. Length 140 mm. Price 9 shillings 6 pence.

693 7.2-inch Howitzer. Length 130 mm. Price 3 shillings 8 pence. Available in olive drab finish.

Price of set 13 shillings 2 pence. Scale 1:59.

No. 697 25-Pounder Field Gun Set

1957–1970. Comprising:

688 Field Artillery Tractor. Length 79 mm. 1962 price 4 shillings 2 pence.

687 Trailer. Length 55 mm. 1962 price 1 shilling 10 pence.

686 25-Pounder Field Gun. Length 8 9 mm. 1962 price 2 shillings 9 pence.

Advertised in *Meccano Magazine* in July 1957 with an issue price of 8 shillings 9 pence. Scale 1:59. Olive drab finish.

No. 698 Tank Transporter and Tank Set

1957–1964. Comprising:

660 Tank Transporter. Issued 1956 to 1964. Folding ramps at rear. Length 337 mm. Price 17 shillings 6 pence. 651 Centurion Tank. Issued 1954 to 1971. Rotating turret, rubber caterpillar tracks running over six pairs of solid wheels, two pairs of rotating wheels with axles. Length 146 mm. Price 7 shillings 11 pence. Price of set 17 shillings 6 pence. Scale 1:59.

No. 699 Military Vehicles Set

1955–1958. Comprising:

621 3-ton Army Wagon. Issued 1954 to 1963. Scale 1:59. Length 115 mm. Price 5 shillings 3 pence.

641 1-ton Cargo Truck. Issued 1954 to 1962. Scale 1:59. Length 79 mm. Price 3 shillings 9 pence.

674 Austin Champ. Issued 1954 to 1970. Scale 1:55. Length 70 mm. Price 3 shillings 6 pence.

676 Armoured Personnel Carrier. Issued 1955 to 1959. Scale 1:48. Length 102 mm. Price 4 shillings 6 pence.

1955 price of set 17 shillings 6 pence.

No. 754 Pavement Set

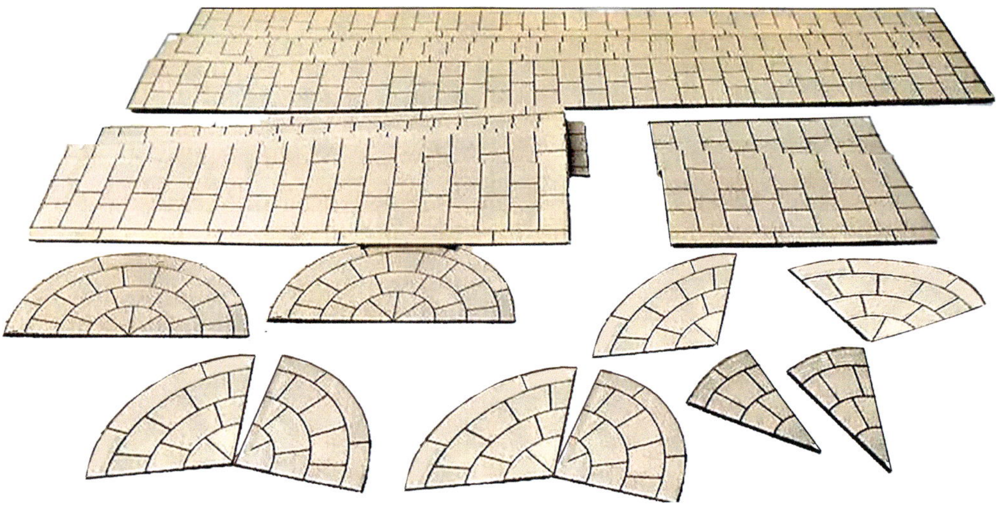

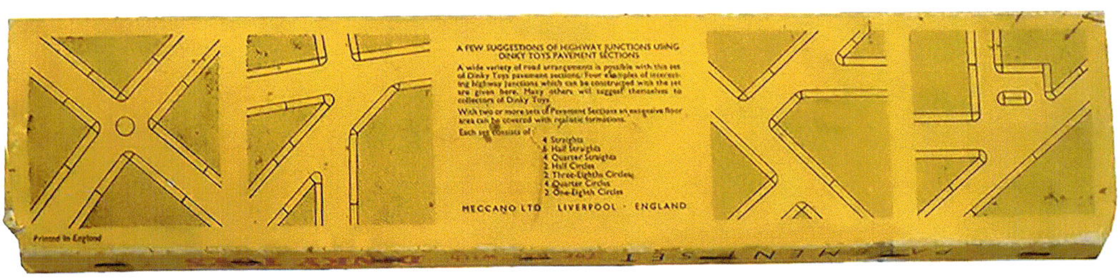

1958–1962. Comprising: four straight lengths, six half-size lengths, four quarter-size lengths, two half-circles, two three-eighth circles, four quarter-circles and two one-eighth circles. Used to make a wide variety of road arrangements and especially when using more than one set. Price 2 shillings 5 pence.

No. 766 British Road Signs Country Set A

1959–1964. Comprising six signs commonly seen in the countryside: Narrow Bridge, Bend (left), Crossing No Gate, Cattle, Crossroads and Road Narrows. Price 2 shillings 8 pence.

No. 767 British Road Signs Country Set B

1959–1964. Comprising six signs commonly seen in the countryside: Bend (right), Level Crossing, Hump Bridge, Hill 1 in 7 and Low Bridge Headroom 14'-0". Price 2 shillings 8 pence.

No. 768 British Road Signs Town Set A

1959–1964. Comprising six signs commonly seen in the town: Roundabout, No Right Turn, Slow Major Road Ahead, Children and No Entry. Price 2 shillings 8 pence.

No. 769 British Road Signs Town Set B

1959–1964. Comprising six signs commonly seen in the town: Halt at Major Road Ahead, No Waiting, Road Junction, School, 30 mph Speed Limit and End of Restriction. Price 2 shillings 8 pence.

No. 771 International Road Signs

1953–1965. Comprising a set of twelve international road signs agreed in Geneva in 1949: Level Crossing Gated, Speed Limit, No Parking, Major Road Ahead, No Overtaking, Dangerous Bend, One Way Road, No Entry, Secondary Road Ahead, Keep Right, Cross Roads Danger, Maximum Weight Permissible, School. Price 3 shillings 9 pence.

No. 772 British Road Signs

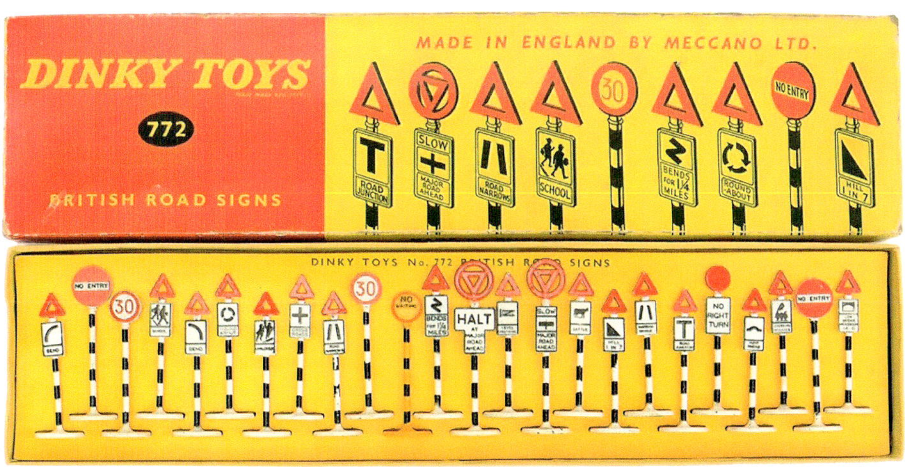

1959–1963. Comprising: Bend (Right), two No Entry, 2 x 30 mph Restriction, School, Bend (Left), Roundabout, Children, Crossroads, Road Narrows, No Waiting, Bends for 1¼ Miles, Halt Major Road Ahead, Slow Major Road Ahead, Level Crossing, Cattle, Hill 1 in 7, Narrow Bridge, Road Junction, No Right Turn, Hump Bridge, Crossing No Gate and Low Bridge Headroom 14'-0". Each sign has a white base and banded poles with relevant signs. Price 10 shillings 6 pence.

No. 778 Road Repair Warning Signs

1962-1963. Comprising: Road Up, No Entry, Danger Road Works Ahead, Keep Left and two Stop and Go reversible signs. Various heights of 30 mm to 40 mm. Price 2 shillings 11 pence.

No. 781 Esso Petrol Pumps Set

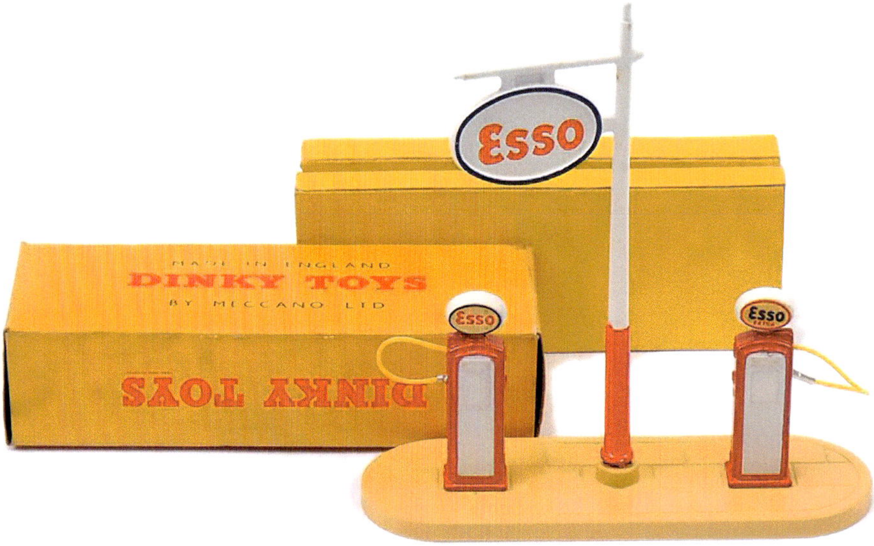

1955–1966. Comprising: advertising standard and two pumps that are detachable from the base. The colours are to the standard Esso design. Height 114 mm. Length 114 mm. Price 2 shillings 11 pence.

No. 782 Shell Petrol Pumps Set

1960–1966. Comprising advertising standard and four pumps that are detachable from the base. The colours are to the standard Shell design. Height 114 mm. Length 203 mm. Price 7 shillings 6 pence.

No. 783 BP Petrol Pumps Set

1960–1966. Comprising advertising standard and four pumps that are detachable from the base. The colours are to the standard BP design. Height 114 mm. Length 203 mm. Price 7 shillings 6 pence.

No. 798 Express Passenger Train (see also 16)

1955–1959. Renumbered from 16, comprising green and black loco with a British Railways logo on the tender, two cream and red carriages on a black chassis. With British Railways livery instead of LNER. Early versions also had a grey roof. Length 302 mm. Price 8 shillings 6 pence.

No. 851 Loads For Lorries

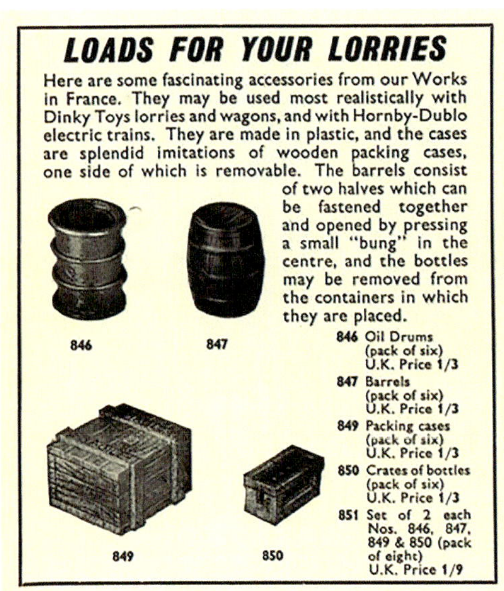

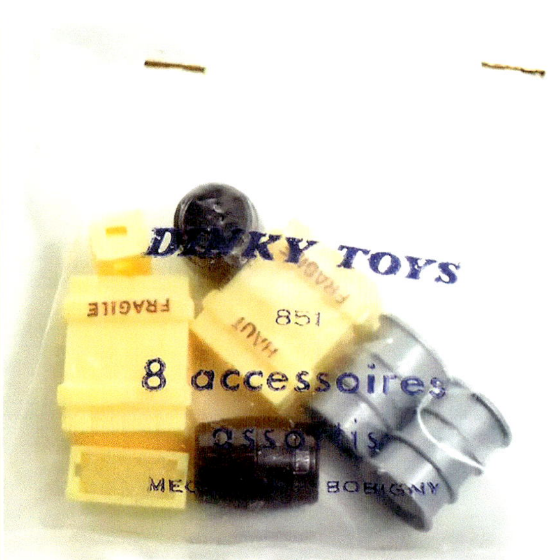

1961–1963. Comprising two each of 846 oil drums, 847 barrels, 849 packing cases, 850 cases of bottles. Price 1 shilling 9 pence.

No. 900 Site Building Set

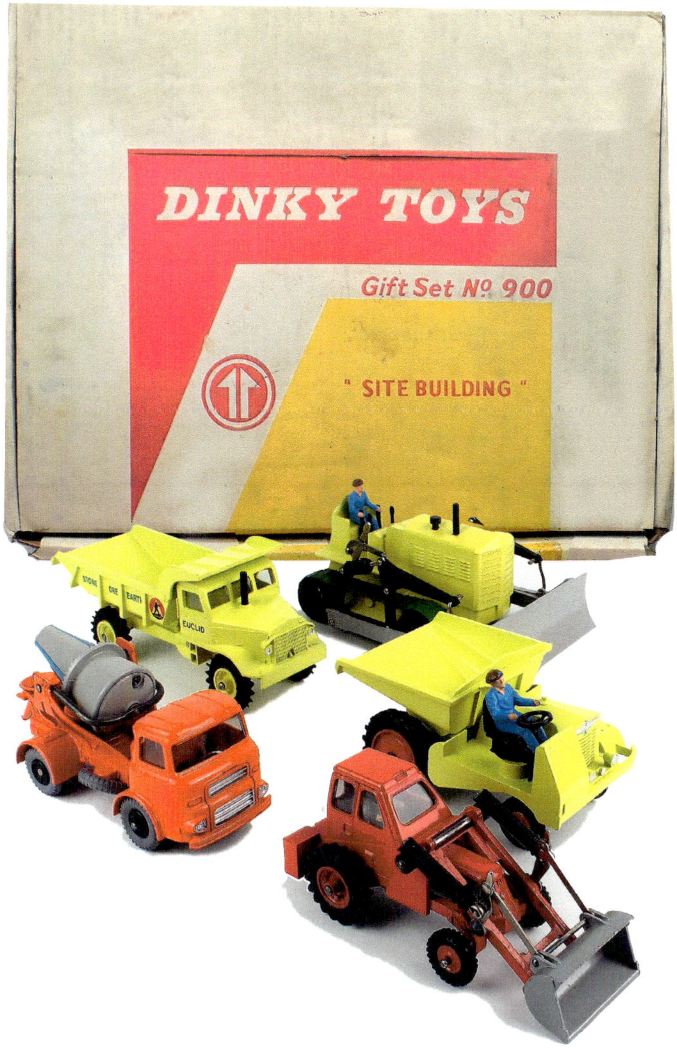

1964–1970. Comprising:

437 Muir Hill 2WL Loader. Red (yellow) body, lever operates the bucket and arm up and down, simulated ram action, windows in cab. Length 120 mm. Price 9 shillings 11 pence.

960 Albion Lorry. Concrete red (orange) body, grey (blue and yellow), cone-shaped, Mixer drum tips and rotates. Length 130 mm. Price 9 shillings 11 pence.

961 Blaw-Knox Bulldozer, yellow (red, orange) body, grey (red, green) blade. Lever operates blade up and down. Creeper tracks. Length 143 mm. Price 12 shillings 6 pence.

962 Muir Hill Dumper Truck, yellow body, adjustable steering, tipping bucket, reversible driver. Length 108 mm. Price 9 shillings 11 pence.

965 Euclid Rear Dump Truck, yellow body, decals Euclid, ore, stone and earth, yellow hubs, lever tips rear to deposit load. Length 143 mm. Price 11 shillings 6 pence.

Price of set 53 shilling 11 pence.

No. 957 Fire Service Set

1961–1964. Comprising:

257 Nash Rambler Fire Chief Car. Length 102 mm. Price 3 shillings 7 pence. 955 Commer Fire Engine, extending ladder, windows, matt black base, red plastic hubs. Length 140 mm. 1961 price 8 shillings 6 pence.

956 Bedford Turntable Fire Escape, extending and rotatable ladder, windows, matt black base, red plastic hubs. Length 197 mm. 1961 price 13 shillings.

Price of set 1 pound 5 shillings.

No. 983 Car Carrier and Trailer

1959–1963. Comprising:

984 car carrier rear ramp lowers, top deck lowered and raised by handle on side. Length 237 mm. Price 1 pound 2 shillings.

985 trailer, rear ramp hinges, front wheels swivel. Length 230 mm. Price 1 pound 2 shillings.

Price of set 1 pound 17 shillings 6 pence.

No. 990 Pullmore Car Transporter Set

1957–1958. Comprising:

982 Pullmore Car Transporter, mid-blue cab, light blue back, 'Dinky Toys Delivery Service' on sides, mid-blue hubs. Length 250 mm. 1956 price 17 shillings 6 pence.

154 Hillman Minx Saloon, light green lower body, cream upper body, beige ridged hubs. Length 87 mm. 1956 price 2 shillings 6 pence.

156 Rover 75 Saloon, blue upper body, cream lower body and ridged hubs. Length 101 mm. 1956 price 3 shillings.

161 Austin Somerset Saloon, yellow upper body, red lower body and ridged hubs. Length 89 mm. 1956 price 2 shillings 6 pence.

162 Ford Zephyr Saloon, light green lower body, cream upper body, beige ridged hubs. Length 96 mm. 1956 price 3 shillings.

794 Loading Ramp. Length 233 mm. 1956 price 1 shilling and 7 pence.

Price of set 1 pound 8 shillings 11 pence.

154 Hillman Minx Saloon

156 Rover 75 Saloon

161 Austin Somerset Saloon

162 Ford Zephyr Saloon

About the Author

Alan Spree BSc CEng MICE MCIHT was born in Nottingham in 1944 and was educated at Glaisdale Bilateral School in Bilborough. He moved to Portsmouth with his family in 1959 and completed his secondary education at Eastney Modern School. He took an apprenticeship as a bricklayer in Portsmouth Dockyard and as part of that he received further education at Highbury Technical College. He then gained a degree in civil engineering at Portsmouth University before becoming a professionally qualified civil engineer. Alan worked with the Department of Environment at Portsmouth, Reading, London and Germany until voluntary retirement in 1998. He then worked for Berkshire County Council and Preston City Council before retirement to Spain in 2006.

His previous Dinky Toys books with Amberley Publishing are:

British Military Dinky Toys (2019)
French Military Dinky Toys (2023)

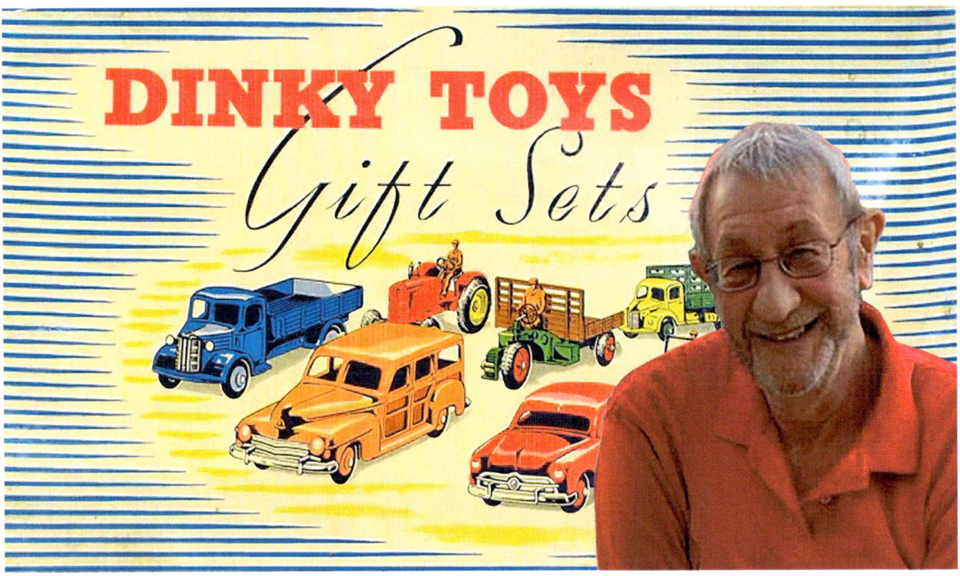